GIUSEPPE LUGLI

THE
ROMAN FORUM
AND THE
PALATINE

WITH 40 ILLUSTRATIONS AND TWO PLATES

BARDI EDITORE – ROMA

THE ROMAN FORUM

——

1. – Introduction.

The inhabitants of the three hills, the Palatine, the Capitoline and the Esquiline, chose the valley lying between them as their common business center and market-place. The points in favour of the site were its central position as regards the three villages which formed the original nucleus of the city, and the ample extent of level ground. Since it lay outside the boundaries of the villages it was called *forum* (fig. 1).

In order to utilize this space, it was first of all necessary to drain it thoroughly and to carry off the waters which rendered it swampy and uninhabitable. The Tarquins are traditionally supposed to have built the great drain, the *Cloaca Maxima*, which crosses the whole valley from North to South, and whose construction marks the beginning of the life of the Roman Forum. The ancients called it simply the Forum or the Great Forum, *Forum Magnum*, to distinguish it from the other Fora, that is to say the Forum Boarium, the Forum

Suarium, the Forum Piscarium and the Forum Holito-
rium. These were respectively the cattle, swine, fish and
vegetable markets: they were established much later and
had much less importance.

The great importance of the Roman Forum even in
the remotest antiquity is proved by traditional accounts
of the most noteworthy events of primitive history: the
Rape of the Sabines, the encounter between Romulus
and Titus Tatius, the meetings of the Senators, the rati-
fication of alliances, etc.

In historic times the Forum was at first the spot
where the farmers and merchants " brought what they
wanted to sell " and thus all around the square, shops
were built for butchers, fruiterers and bankers. The
central space and the *Comitium* were used for political
and sacred functions, for the election of magistrates, the
hearing of law-suits, the publication of edicts, the principal religious ceremonies, the public games, and all those
other ceremonies that formed part of civic life.

At first they all used to take place in the open air;
later special halls were built, first in wood and later in
masonry (*tabernae*). Then the first Basilicas the Porcia,
the Sempronia and the Aemilia, were founded, while at
the northern end of the Comitium was placed the *Curia*
for the meetings of the Senate. At an earlier date the
chief sanctuaries in the Forum were dedicated to gods:
that of Vesta, the heart of the City, of Janus, of Saturn,
of the Castors, the protectors of the Roman legions, of

Fig. 1. – General view of the Roman Forum from the Arch of Titus.

Concord, of Venus Cloacina which was situated near the Cloaca Maxima. Proper roads were built to facilitate communications with the other parts of the city; the *Vicus Tuscus* with the Velabrum, the *Clivus Argentarius* with the Campus Martius and the *Argiletum* with the Esquiline.

Thus in the period between the 3rd and 2nd centuries B. C., the Forum had already become a stately square surrounded by monumental buildings, and was the center of all the life of the city, both public and private. Plautus, in the *Curculio*, thus describes the appearance of the great square (trans. Nixou, Loeb):

" I will show you where you can readily find men of every variety, so that no one will have to labour too laboriously if he wished to meet anyone vicious of virtuous, worthy or worthless. If you wish to meet a perjurer, go to the Comitium; for a liar and a braggart, try the Temple of Venus Cloacina; for wealthy married waters, the Basilica. There too will be harlots, well ripened ones, and men ready for a bargain, while at the fish-market are the members of eating clubs. In the lower Forum citizens of repute and wealthy stroll about; in the middle Forum, near the Canal, there you find the merely showy set. Above the *Lacus* (Curtius) are those brazen, garrulous, spiteful fellows who boldly decry other people without reason and are open to plentry of truthful criticism themselves. Below the Old Shops are those who lend and borrow upon usury. Behind the Temple of Castor are those whom you would do ill to trust too quickly. In the Tuscan quarter are those worthies who sell themselves: in the Velabrum bakers, butchers, soothsayers, either those who turn themselves or give others a chance to turn ".

But the Forum was not merely a meeting place. At the time of the Gracchi, of Sulla, of the two Triumvirates, it became the scene of violent struggles, its venerable buildings were turned into fortresses often with disastrous results. Thus the Forum was several times rebuilt, especially under Sulla and Caesar. The latter indeed conceived the plan of general reconstruction which was completed by Augustus. The Forum, the scene of Caesar's triumphs, was fittingly enough his tomb. His body was burned near the *Via Sacra* in front of the Temple of the Dioscuri, and Augustus built on the spot the *Templum Divi Iulii*.

At the time of Augustus the Temples of the Castors and of Concord, the Basilica Aemilia and the *Regia* were entirely rebuilt, a new basilica (the Iulia) was founded on the site of the older Basilica Sempronia, the Curia of the Senate was moved, in accordance with Caesar's plan, to where it now stands, and new arches and honorary monuments were raised.

Under the Empire the Forum lost its former importance. The center of public life moved to the newer Imperial Fora which were more spacious and comfortable, while the Forum was left to be peopled by monuments (fig. 2). The Emperor took care to enlarge it by adding an area on the East side right up to the Arch of Titus, which they embellished with porticos and honorary monuments. For a short time Nero at first had devoted this space to the immense portico which was to be the entrance to his Golden House, but it was soon swept away. Domitian, Trajan and Hadrian rebuilt all that part of the Forum which lay under the Palatine, renewing the *Via Nova* which bounded it on the South.

On this occasion the House of the Vestals and the Temple of Vesta were reconstructed, and a monumental entrance to the Imperial Palace on the Palatine (the so-called Temple of Augustus) was created.

For a few years it came to life again under Maxentius and Constantine, the former building the temple of Romulus on the *Via Sacra* and beginning the great Basilica, while the latter placed the seven honorary columns and his own equestrian statue in the area of the Forum itself, in front of the Basilica Julia. But on the removal of the seat of the Empire the Forum started on its rapid decline. The first blow was struck by the edicts of Constants (346 A.D.) and Gratian (383 A.D.) ordering all pagan temples to be closed, thus hastening their ruin: but far graver were the Gothic and Vandal invasion in 410 and 455 A. D. when many buildings were destroyed, including the Curia. Then the Christians took them over and built their churches in the ruins of the temples.

Fig. 2. – View of the Roman Forum from the Capitol.

The last memorial in the classical Forum is the column named in honour of Phocas, Emperor of the East, for having given the Pope the Pantheon, that it might be dedicated to the Virgin. But already in the 8th century the various buildings were crumbling one by one; heaps of ruins blocked the streets and were turned to good account by all who needed building material. Frequent earthquakes, and especially the famous one under Leo 4th, increased the ruin and desolation. Everything valuable or of use was carried elsewhere and used especially in building new churches. The remains gradually spread and raised the level of the valley, while more earth and ruins were washed down the steep slopes of the surrounding hills (fig. 3). Thus in the middle ages the level of the Forum had risen to that of the modern street which crosses it, and while the capitals of the temples which surrounded it still appeared above ground, the column of Phocas alone marked the site of the square itself.

The Roman Forum had become a field for the pasturage of cattle — whence its name *Campo Vaccino* — who were watered at a fountain near the temple of the Castors, formed out of a large cup of granite, now used for the fountain in front of the Quirinal Palace. A wide road, lined with a double row of elms, united the Arches of Titus and Septimius Severus, while a few houses stood above the Comitium and the Basilica Aemilia.

So remained the Forum until the 17th century, when Pius 6th and Gregory 16th undertook the first excavations

Fig. 3. – The Roman Forum in the 17th century.

which were subsequently continued by the Italian Government under the main direction of Rodolfo Lanciani and Giacomo Boni.

2. – THE MONUMENTS OT THE FOOT OF THE CAPITOL.

Before entering the Forum itself, it will be well to have a look at the buildings which are cut off from the rest by the modern road.

The **Carcer.** (No 1 on Plan I). The entrance is in front of the little church to the right of the steps leading up to the Capitol. The wall to the left of the stairs by which we descend is the facade of the building known in late times as the Mamertine Prison. Its name in classic times was *Tullianum*, not from king Servius Tullius, but from the word *tullus* meaning a spring. The wall is built of large and well squared blocks of tufa internally and of travertine externally with round holes for crowbars; above these runs a band of travertine bearing the names of Caius Vibius Rufinus and M. Cocceius Nerva, the two consuls who built it, perhaps in the reign of Tiberius.

At the foot of the modern stairs the original door leads into the upper room of the prison. It is trapezoidal in shape and is covered by a vault, formed of regular blocks of tufa, forming a round arch that has been partly cut into on the left owing to the irregular plan of the room.

We descend the modern stairs into the lower room, circular in shape but later cut through on one side by a straight wall on which the facade of the building rests. Originally it was a water-cistern, like the one near the House of Augustus on the Palatine. Only three rings of the vaulting exist at present, all of tufa masonry.

There is nothing to prove that it was covered with a corbelled dome, but it is certain that, before the present flat stone ceiling, it had a wooden roof. Holes for the beams, which were afterwards closed up with stones and mortar, can still be seen on the walls, and this roof was probably used as a centering on which to lay the vaulting.

The original circular wall consisted of three rows of blocks and, even before the construction of the vault, it had been cut by a transverse wall which was later used as a foundation for the room above. It is difficult to date these numerous alterations. The *tholos*, though considered by some only of the 3rd century B. C., was certainly earlier and it was probably altered about 200 B. C.

The proof that it was built at first as a cistern is to be found in the little well of fresh water, near the altar, which the legend ascribes to a miracle of St. Peter. On the straight wall an iron door leads to a drain with a transverse arm, which leads to the *Cloaca Maxima*. It carries off the overflow from the well, by means of a channel under the floor, and was also used to remove the bodies of executed prisoners.

In antiquity the entrance was through a hole in the roof, and here were thrown the greatest political prisoners of the Roman Republic, who were left to starve to death or to await the executioner. Sallust, in mentioning the imprisonment and execution here of the members of the Catilinarian conspiracy, well describes the terrible appearance of the chamber: the darkness, the dampness, and the unbearable stench of dead bodies. Here Vercingetorix was thrown, and here Jugurtha " for six days struggling with hunger, and to the very last minute desirous of life, was overtaken by the just reward of his villanies " (Plutarch). Upon being cast naked into the dungeon he is said to have cried out with a ghastly laugh, " O Hercules! How cold your bath is! " For less guilty or less dangerous criminals there existed near by less dreadful prisons called *lautumiae*, probably old quarries at the foot of the hill.

Following the road across the Forum the first monument on the right, immediately after the Capitol steps, is the base and foundations of the **Temple of Concord,** (Plan, n. 2), built by Tiberius in 10 A. D. during the reign of Augustus with the proceeds of the booty from Germany. Camillus had originally dedicated it in 367 B.C. to mark the end of the long struggles between the Patricians and the People. It was so badly demaged during the Civil War in the time of the Gracchi, that it had to be rebuilt in stone, having been formerly built of wood covered with terracotta plaques in the Etruscan fashion. Owing to the numerous gifts it received, especially from Livia, the wife of Augustus, it grew to be a regular museum, and contained pictures and sculptures of the most celebrated Greek artists (fig. 4).

Because of the restricted space between the *Tabularium* and the *Clivus Capitolinus* (which ran more or less

Fig. 4. – The Temple of Concord
on a coin of Tiberius.

on the line of the modern road), Tiberius was obliged to make the *Cella* of the Temple much wider than the depth. On the long side towards the Forum was the entrance under an extensive projecting portico with ten Corinthian columns. The remains consist of: the concrete *podium*, supported by great tufa walls on which rose the Temple

itself, a portion of the stairway in front, and the threshold
of the door – two great slabs of *porta santa* marble, on one
of which is sculptured a *caduceus*, the attribute of Mercury
once filled with bronze. Part of the cornice of the Temple
is preserved in the Tabularium.

The three magnificent columns which follow belong
to the corner of the hexastyle portico of the **Temple of
Vespasian** (Plan no. 3). It was raised to that Emperor's
memory by his two sons Titus and Domitian, when on
the death of Vespasian in 79 A. D. he was proclaimed
Divus. Titus died only two years later, and so the Temple
was dedicated to his memory as well, and indeed at the
end of the *Cella* can be seen the wide base that supported
the statues of the two Emperors. The fragmentary
inscription on the cornice refers to a restoration of the
Temple by Septimius Severus and Caracalla. On the
frieze are the various sacerdotal insignia of the Pontifex
Maximus, a dignity which Vespasian possessed as Emperor.

The last building on the right it the **Porticus of the
Dii Consentes,** (Plan no. 4) which was largely rebuilt in
1858 with the fragments which had been found in 1834.
The building is curiously shaped, since it is formed by
two arms of a cipollino colonnade which meet at an obtuse
angle, onto which opened twelve rooms, now only seven.
Varro mentions the gilt bronze statues of the 12 Gods
(Jupiter, Juno, Neptune, Minerva, Mars, Venus, Apollo,
Diana, Mercury, Cerer, Vulvan and Vesta) as existing

in his day, but there are no remains of the Temple of that era. What we see to-day is the result of a complete reconstruction which, from the brickwork, appears to have been executed under the Flavians, and was later enlarged and modified as we know from the inscription on the architrave, by the Prefect of the City, Vettius Agorius Praetextatus in 367 A. D. It is probable that he rebuilt it according to the primitive plan.

Between the Porticus of the Dii Consentes and the Temple of Saturn (Plan, no 20) runs the street which led up to the summit of the Capitol, in front of the Temple of Jupiter. After the settlement of this side of the hill, carried out by the Municipality of Rome, the pavement in flintstone has reappeared almost in its entirety. The recent excavations show that it follows a rectilinear, very sloping direction quite different from the one expected.

3. — THE COMITIUM AND THE STREET OF JANUS.

We will now enter the area of the Forum proper from the entrance at the end of the Via Cavour. The modern path runs between the Temple of Antoninus and Faustina to the left and the **Basilica Aemilia** to the right (Plan no. 5), into which we descend.

This was one of the most ancient Basilicas in Rome, famous for the mignificence with which it had been decorated, and several times restored by members of one family, the *gens Aemilia*, who had charge of it till late in

Imperial times. There are but scanty remains left, in which, however, one can distinguish three different periods: to the earliest period, that of its foundation in 179 B. C. by the censor M. Fulvius Nobilior and M. Aemilius Lepidus, belong a few walls made of small blocks of tufa, which were incorporated in the later construction. To L. Aemilius Paullus (55-54 B. C.) is due most of the building, which was slightly restored in 14 and 22. A. D. under Tiberius. Lastly the work done in the time of Honorius is easily distinguished by the use of brick to strengthen the walls after the building had been set on fire in 410 A. D. during the Gothic invasion.

It much resembled the Basilica Julia which stood opposite on the other side of the Forum. A great double-storied portico ran all along the front and was decorated with gilded shields placed here by the consul M. Aemilius Lepidus. Inside this portico was a row of *tabernae*, or shops, which are still in a good state of preservation. Behind the *tabernae* was the great hall, now almost entirely razed to the ground, which was formerly divided into aisles by means of pilasters. There was first an aisle 5 metres in width; then came the great nave, about 12 metres wide and 80 metres long, richly paved with coloured marbles: *cipollino*, *giallo antico*, *portasanta*, etc. Two smaller aisles or passages completed the building on the side towards the Forum of Nerva.

The interior also consisted of two stories. To the first story belong the beautiful marble pilasters carved with acanthus spirals in bas relief, and the big fragments of columns of *africano* marble which are scattered all over the area; to the second a cornice with acanthus decoration which can be seen in the portico. The style of all these fragments proves them to belong to the reconstruction by Tiberius. It is not certain to what part of the building belonged the marble slabs (decorated with deep-cut acanthus spirals, from which emerge some fantastic monsters), that are hung on the wall of a mediaeval building on the eastern side of the Basilica.

The entablature of the outer portico, in the Tuscan order of architecture, was decorated with *boukrania* which led to the supposition in Renaissance times that this was the site of the Forum Boarium. On the pavement of the nave can still be seen some coins that fused together with the bronze decoration during the fire in 410 A. D. and stuck to the marble slabs. In a corner, near the entrance to the Forum, part of the upper frieze of the *Cella* has been reconstructed, with reliefs representing scenes from the primitive history of Rome.

The portico was restored in late Imperial times and traces of this restoration are the three granite columns that have been replaced on their pedestals during the course of the recent excavations (Plan, A.). Among the mass of ruins that lie near the S. E. corner of the Basilica may be seen fragments of a great marble revetment bearing a dedicatory inscription to Lucius Caesar, adopted as son by Augustus together with Caius Caesar. Both died young, not without suspicion of poison administered by order of Livia.

Before leaving the Basilica Aemilia we should glance at a little round substructure of travertine with a marble rim (Plan, 7). It is usually supposed to have been the **Sacellum Cloacinae,** a shrine of Venus, called Cloacina since it stood near the point where the *Cloaca Maxima* enters the Forum. It is reproduced on some coins minted under the second Triumvirate.

At the Western end of the Basilica Aemilia is usually placed the site of the *Temple of Janus* (Plan, J.). This was a tiny square sanctuary, with two doors at either end, the whole covered with bronze slabs. The statue of Janus Bifrons in the interior was also of bronze, and was 2.50 metres high. This sanctuary, which was still in existence in the sixth century. A. D., has entirely disappeared, and probably stood on the spot where later was built a square mediaeval tower of brick (Plan, C.).

The area beyond the road called the *Argiletum,* [between the *Curia* (9), the Arch of Septimius Severus (14) and the *Lapis Niger* (10)] is all that was left in Imperial times of the public **Comitium** the place where the representatives of the 30 *Curiae,* (into which the population of the city was politically divided) met to discuss and vote the laws, to elect the magistrates, and to exercise in certain penal cases the powers of a Court of Appeal. The *Comitium* was separated from the Forum proper which lay on the south, and, although under the Empire the

Fig. 5. – The Curia of the Roman Senate
after the restoration.

two areas had been almost united, each had its own individual character. The complicated stratification that is to be seen in the ancient pavement, going from the earliest Republican to the latest Imperial times, shows how busy was the life of this small spot, the center of the political life of Rome during the free times of the Republic.

In front of the *Comitium* stands the **Curia,** the meeting place of the Senate, which, together with the popular assembly of the *Comitia*, constituted the executive power of the Roman state under the Republic, whence the necessity for the places being close together. Tradition stated that the first Senate House had been built by Tullis Hostilius (*Curia Hostilia*). Enlarged and embellished by Sulla, this venerable building was burned down in 52 B. C. during the riots that took place at the funeral of Clodius. It was orientated North and South like all the most ancient monuments in the Comitium. In 44 B. C. Caesar began the reconstruction which was called after him *Curia Julia* and was only finished fifteen years later by Augustus, who dedicated a large statue of Victory in the interior.

It was again restored by Domitian and its appearance at that time may be judged from the representation of the *Anaglypha* (No. 15). But it was again burned in the fire under Carinus and was rebuilt in its present form by Diocletian (fig. 5). The hall (25.20 + 17.60 m.) was transformed in the Middle Ages into the Church of St. Adriano, while to the left, the Church of St. Martina is built on the site of the room where the archives of the

Senate were kept (the *Secretarium Senatus*). Between the two halls, in the space now occupied by the modern *Bia Bonella*, was a great square courtyard (*Chalcidicum*) built by Augustus and dedicated by Domitian to Minerva, whence the name *Atrium Minervae*.

The importance attributed by antiquity to the *Curia* of the Roman Senate made it advisable, during the last years, to demolish the baroque Church of St. Adrian in order to bring the ancient building back to its original condition. Under the pavement of the Church, the former one of Diocletian's epoch has been discovered. It is a very fine work in colored marbles with geometrical and ornamental drawings. Furthermore, beside the longer sides, have been found the steps upon which the senatorial chairs were placed. At the bottom, the presidential scaffold with the base supporting the famous statue of the *Victoria*, reappeared. The longer walls are each decorated with three niches, like little altars, with marble columns and spandrels. Also the lower portion of the wall was coated with marble, while the upper portion was in stucco-work. Two openings in the bottom wall lead to a little yard where a colossal porphyry statue has been found. The *Anaglypha Traiani*, two large bas-reliefs found in the middle of the Forum, have been temporarily placed in the interior of the Curia, not far from the *Lapis Niger*.

These sculptured **Plutei or Anaglypha** (15), according to current opinion, were executed by order of

Trajan to commemorate two important acts of his reign
which are depicted on the reliefs. On the one nearest
the Arch of Severus, the Emperor is shown instituting a
special fund for the education and support of poor children and orphans; on the other remitting arrears of taxes
from the Roman provinces and borning the *tabulae* on
which they were recorded. The special interest of these
reliefs lies in the fact that the various buildings of the
Forum are represented on them. On the first relief
(fig. 6) we see from left to right: an arch of the *Tabularium* or a triumphal arch destroyed by Septimius Severus;
then the *Curia*, with a pillared facade as it was before
Diocletian's reconstruction; then in front of these two
buildings the *Rostra*, from which the Emperor is address-
ing the people; then an open space (the *Argiletum*) followed by the *Basilica Aemilia*, closing, with its long portico,
that side of the Forum, in the center of which is a symbolic group depicting the Emperor receiving the homage of
Italy and the children; lastly the scene is closed by the
ficus ruminalis and by the statue of Marsyas holding a wine
skin, both of which stood in the center of the Forum.

The second relief shows the other side of the Forum,
beginning where the other left off, with the *ficus* and the
Marsyas; then comes the *Basilica Julia*, also with its long
Doric portico; then the Temple of Saturn; then another
arch, perhaps that of Tiberius, followed by the Temple
of Vespasian, while the scene must have been closed by
the Temple of Concord, represented on the missing slab.

Fig. 6. – Imperial relief with buildings of the Roman Forum in the background.
(Arcus; Curia. Argiletum. Basilica Aemilia. Marsyas.)

On the inner side of each relief is represented the solemn sacrifice of the *Souvetaurilia* (of a pig, a sheep and a bull), offered by the people in gratitude for Trajan's philanthropic measures.

These two reliefs were perhaps used as decorative panels on each side of the parapet of the *Rostra*, while Boni supposes them to have decorated a *Tribunal Traiani*. In late Imperial times they were taken down and used to decorate an honorary base in the area of the Forum, near the place where they stand today.

At the foot of the Curia steps, part of a flat circular basin of marble with a moulded edge and an octagonal space in the center (8) may be seen in the pavement of the *Comitium*. This formed part of a fountain and perhaps supported the big granite basin which forms part of the fountain in front of the Quirinal Palace, and which during the Middle Ages stood near the Temple of the Castors and was fed by the Spring of Juturna.

We will now turn to examine the oldest and most important monument in the Forum, the famous **Lapis Niger** (fig. 7), which is now protected by a roof. It is probable that this almost square area was paved with six rows of black marble blocks in expiation of the violation of some of the most sacred Roman monuments xhich had taken place at some time or another. Under this black stone, legend placed the Tomb of Romulus, the founder of the city, or the tomb of Hostus, the grandfather of Tullus Hostilius, decorated with two lions. The excavations of 1899 brought to light a square foundation which may well belong to a sepulcher, and two bases that could be exactly utilized to suppert two crouching lions. Under the pavement there are also a truncated cone of

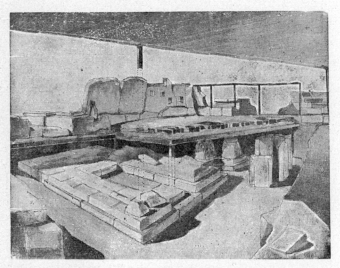

Fig. 7. – The Lapis Niger on the Comitium.

tufa and a broken pyramidal stele. On all four faces of the latter runs a vertical inscription which goes from the top down and from the bottom up, a form of writing known as *boustrophedon*. This finely cut inscription is the oldest existing Latin document, but unfortunately its interpretation, despite numerous attempts, is still uncertain. The only words completely preserved are RECEI (*rex*-king) KALATOREM (an official engaged in the sacrificial ceremonies) (IOUXMENTA (*iumenta*-beasts of burden) and SAKROS ESED (*sacer esto*), which show it to be part of a sacred law and confirms the Roman tradition, by taking us back more or less to the period of the Kings.

The excavations moreover unearthed a considerable number of bronze and pottery statuettes, vase fragments, bones of animals and a large mass of ashes, pointing to the fact that at some time a great sacrifice had taken place. The general plan of the monument shows that the black pavement was laid in the times of Caesar, although this part of the Forum has yet to be studied properly. The black stone is fenced in by big blocks of travertine with a groove into which fitted upright marble slabs, some of which are still in position.

Between the *Lapis Niger* and the *Rostra* is a large marble base for a column (12. It was found in 1547 in front of the *Curia*, where a nother, afterwards destroyed, had been found in 1490. This one also suffered considerable damage, especially the lower part, but the scenes in relief which decorated it can still be distinguished. The front is turned towards the Senate-House and bears an inscription of Diocletian in commemoration of the decennial games of 303 A. D. On the right side are the solemn preparations for the sacrifice of the *souvetaurilia* (the sacrifice of a pig, a sheep and a bull, *sus, ovis, taurus*).

On the left the Emperor is offering a triumphal sacrifice to Mars, the nude figure on the left, and to Rome, the seated figure on the right. The fourth side has a procession of nine persons.

On the same line, just in front of the *Lapis Niger*, stands a high marble block, originally the base of an equestrian statue, as may be seen by the holes on the left side. It was set up in its present position, according to the inscription, in honor of Arcadius and Honorius for a victory over the Goths. Although the name of the general has been erased, it must refer to Stilicho's victory over Radagaisus at Pollentia in 403 A. D.

As we have seen, all this part of the Forum was almost entirely rebuilt in late Imperial times and we have thus lost invaluable material for the history of the Forum and of Rome itself in earliest times. To the latest period must be also attributed the base of the equestrian statue of Constantius that lies between the modern embankment and the Arch of Severus (13). The base itself, a monolith of white marble, rests on a brick foundation, originally also covered with marble, and bears the inscription of Neratius Cerealis, prefect of the city in 353 A. D., who dedicated it.

4. – THE NORTH-WEST SIDE OF THE FORUM.

The first monument on this side is the **Arch of Septimius Severus** (14), dedicated in about 200 A. D. to him and to his two sons, Caracalla and Geta in gratitude

for the victories they had gained over the Arabs and the
Parthians in Mesopotamia (fig. 8). These wars and
victories are depicted in four great pictures above the
smaller passages, while the lunettes on either side of
the arches are filled with winged victories and personific-
ations of rivers (among others the Tigris and the Euph-
rates)' Oner the top of the decorative columns are reliefs
depicting Arab prisoners dragged in chains by the Romans.
In the dedicatory inscription on the attic the name of
Geta in the fourth line has been erased and honorary
titles substituted.

These reliefs already show artistic decadence and we
can clearly see conscious imitation of those on the Antonine and Trajan Columns. The artist — instead of
excuting great compositions like those of the Arch of
Titus, the Arch of Trajan at Beneventum, and the Trajanic and Antonine reliefs on the Arch of Constantine — has
composed a series of pictures on a lesser scale, filled with
smaller figures, so that the limitations of his ability might
be less noticeable. Representations of the arch on coins
and medals show it to have been surmounted by a great
six-horsed chariot, bearing the images of the Emperor and
his two sons, while the holes to be seen on the sides seem
to have supported shields and other ornaments in bronze.
The decoration of the vaulting under the arches is very
interesting, with its rich and carefully sculptured coffering.

The monument was really more commemorative than
triumphal. Thus it was at first raised above the level

Fig. 8. – The Arch of Septimius Severus.

3

of the *Comitium* by means of a wide flight of steps, and only later was it crossed by a road that joined the *Clivus Capitolinus*. Its excellent preservation is due to the fact that during the Middle Ages it was enclosed by the Church of SS. Sergius and Bacchus to the South and by fortifications to the North.

We shall now examine on the NW side of the square the famous **Rostra,** the platform used by the political orators (Plan, no. 16, and fig. 9), so called because the front was decorated with the prows (*rostra*) taken from the enemy's ships at the battle of Antium, 338 B. C., during the Latin war. From its representation on the reliefs of the Arch of Constantine we know that it was also decorated with honorary columns and statues of which the most important was the one of Augustus.

The *Rostra* were moved here from the *Comitium* by Julius Caesar, while Augustus, as we know from the coins, built in 42 B. C. the fine marble hemicycle which forms its back and which is furnished with a wide flight of steps giving access to the platform. The straight part which forms the front has been much restored in modern times with a wall made of small tufa fragments, which exactly copies the ancient wall, formed of blocks of tufa, some few courses of which can be seen at the base. This facade is later than the age of Caesar and is due to an enlargement of the original *Rostra*.

At each extremity of the hemicycle at the back, stood two very interesting monuments. The first, the **Umbi-**

Fig. 9. – Frieze of the Arch of Constantine.
An imperial address from the *Rostra*.

licus Urbis Romae (n. 17), a small round structure of
brick, marked the ideal center of the city, in imitation
of the *omphaloi* that stood in Greek cities. It was probably built under Septimius Severus. The other, the
Miliarium Aureum (n. 18), was a column on which were
written in letters of gold the distances, from Rome, of the
different provinces of the Empire. It was set up by
Augustus in 20 B. C. when he took over the *cura viarum*.
Some fragments of this marble column, 1.20 metres
in diameter, and of its base, decorated with palmettes
in relief (perhaps a 3rd century restoration) are to be seen
at the foot of the Temple of Saturn near their original
position. An iron roof placed behind the *Rostra* covers
the spot where, ever since the age of Romulus, there stood
the altar of Vulcano, the **Volcanal** (n. 19). Two trees
(a lotus and a cypress), said to be older than the city itself,
could also be seen there, at least in republican times.
There were also a bronze *quadriga* dedicated by Romulus,
a statue of Romulus himself, another of Horatius Cocles,
and other venerable records of legendary times.

The area of the Volcanal (3.95 m + 2.80) was bounded
by a tufa wall made of blocks quarried on the spot, while
the altar itself was made of the native rock, which, owing
to the nature of the ground, tends to rise in this spot.

Let us now examine the massive building that stands
before us, at the foot of the Capitoline Hill. This is the
famous **Temple of Saturn** (Plan, n. 20) originally one of
the oldest in Rome. It stands on a lofty *podium* within

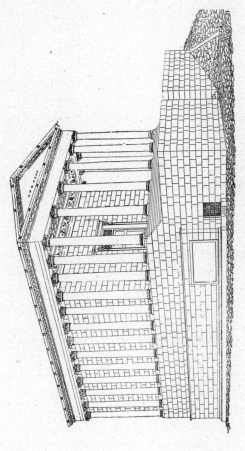

Fig. 10. – Reconstruction of the Temple of Saturnus with the Aerarium arranged in the podium.

whose vaults was kept the public treasury (*Aerarium publicum Populi Romani*). The construction of this foundation (fig. 10) is due to Q. Munatius Plancus, aedile in 42 B. C., but the imposing portico, with its six Ionic columns of grey granite on the front and one on each side, is a 4th century A. D. reconstruction. According to the inscription on the architrave it was due to a fire: *Senatus Populusque Romanus incendio consumptum restituit*. In this reconstruction, however, considerable use was made of the original columns and especially of the fragments of the entablature. The cornice appears to be chieflly Augustan, with some pieces of Trajanic work. Its plan is reproduced on three fragments of the *Forma Urbis* (nn. 22, 23, 30). The very ancient cult statue in the cella is said to have been filled with oil and bound around with wool, and used to be carried about the city during the Triumphal festivals.

5. – THE LAST SECTION ON THE VIA SACRA.

In front of the Temple of Saturn a row of low arches of the republican period should be noticed. They were used as substructures for the *Clivus Capitolinus*, that went right around the Temple, passed under the modern road, then turned sharply behind the Portico of the *Dii Consentes*, winding its way up the hill to the Temple of Jupiter.

The *Clivus Capitolinus* in really a continuation of the VIA SACRA that divided the area of the Forum priper from the *Basilica Julia* (n. 22). This road started from the Velia, where stands the Arch of Titus, and was called *Sacred* because, according to tradition, it had been the scene of the solemn reconciliation between Romulus and the Sabine King Titus Tatius. The real origin of the name is probably to be found in the fact that all the most important sanctuaries stood along it: the Temple of Vesta with the House of the Vestals; that of the Lares; and the *Regia Pontificis*, the residence of the *Pontifex Maximus*. The oldest part of the *Via Sacra* was that between the Velia and the Temple of Castor. In late Imperial times the portion between the Arch of Titus and the Arch of Constantine was added as well as the part between the Temples of Castor, and of Saturn. There were special names for each portion of the road: the highest point, at the Arch of Titus, was called the *Summa Sacra Via* or *Clivus Sacer*; the part up to the Temple of Caesar was called the *Media Sacra Via*; and the last bit in the Forum was the *Ima Sacra Via*. The middle portion is the one best preserved today at the original Augustan level, which was afterwards raised, first by Nero, and later by Constantine when he built the new entrance to the great Basilica. Remains of the pavement of that age are still to be seen at those points where the embankment has been left at that height.

At the end of the road, where it begins to rise towards the Capitol, are the concrete foundations of the **Arch of Tiberius** (n. 21 on Plan), in an excavation to the right of the Way. It was composed of a single arch, and was built about 16 A. D. in honor of Tiberius and Germanicus who had recaptured the standards which the Germans had taken from the legions that had been defeated under Varus. It is shown on the frieze of the arch of Constantine (fig. 10).

We will now mount the steps that run along the whole length of this portion of the Sacred Way and the *Vicus Tuscus*, and visit the **Basilica Julia,** (n. 22), the largest in the Forum. It has been almost entirely destroyed, and the only remains are the pavement of the central hall, some travertine piers which have been reconstructed, and some rooms at the back, still partly buried under the modern road.

The brick piers which stand around the central hall are all due to a modern reconstruction, but follow the ancient plan of the Basilica, that consisted of a large rectangular hall in the center, surrounded by a portico with two stories. Another two-storied portico, formed of arches and piers with engaged columns, decorated the front of the building towards the Sacred Way and the *Vicus Tuscus*.

The original Basilica was built by Julius Caesar for the hearing of civil cases, and was dedicated by him in 46 B. C. It was destroyed by fire under Augustus, who then rebuilt it throughout. Other fires took place under Carinus (284 A. D.) and Diocletian (305 A. D.), and the Basilica was restored for the last time by the prefect of the city, Vettius Probianus, in 416 A. D.

6. – THE AREA OF THE FORUM.

We now descend from the Basilica Julia and after crossing again the *Ima Sacra Via* and passing in front of some large brick bases of columns, we enter the *Forum* proper, the real square of Rome. Its boundaries were: the *Rostra* (16), the *Lapis Niger* (10), the *Basilica Aemilia* (5), the Temple of Julius Caesar (28), the Arch of Augustus (29), the Temple of Castor (30), and the Basilica Julia (22). Even in the last days of the Republic the space was still almost completely free and was the meeting place of the whole population of the city. But under the Empire it lost its original character and was gradually filled up by monuments, which reduced the open space available and rendered it simply an official and formal center. The life of the city moved over to the Imperial Fora, more spacious and suitable for the great ceremonies of the capital of the Empire; but in Republican times, all the ceremonies, all important discussions, all public meetings took place in the Forum. Here the innumerable loiterers used to meet while the farmers negotiated their contracts. On the *Rostra* were discussed the civil cases in the presence of the whole populace. The *praetor*, seated on his tribunal, pronounced legal decisions that were afterwards published and affixed to the walls of the neighboring rostra, together with the proscription lists, with the various magistrates' edicts, and with other official communications.

All the more important sacrifices, especially in times of danger, and all the principal religious festivals took place in the Forum. Sometimes even the sacred banquets and the prayers of expiation were held here. Through the Forum passed the solemn procession, the *pompa triumphalis* and the *pompa circensis*. Often it was the scene of the execution of political offenders, of gladiatorial spectacles and of the funerals of illustrious personages, especially if their death had been due to violence, as was the case for Clodius and Julius Caesar. Then what was almost a separate world of foreigners practically lived in the Forum near the Basilica Aemilia, together with the merchants who came from the furthest corners of the Empire, dressed in their strange native costumes, all mingling with the motley crowd, intent on business or politics, ready to applaud a famous orator or a mountebank, or bribed to break up a meeting or to support a new politician or party.

Seven large Bases (23) stand on the edge of the Forum, skirting the Via Sacra. Built of brickwork of poor quality, they supported columns, some portions of which have been set up while other fragments lie scattered about near by. On these columns stood statues of various important individuals who had deserved the State's special gratitude in the time of Diocletian. Apparently something of this kind existed even before that time, since inside the brickwork of some of them have been found traces of large pilasters of masonry.

Of the monuments of the Forum the most conspicuous and significant is certainly the **Column of Phocas** (24). It stands on a lofty brick base surrounded by steps, and is a memorial of the gratitude of Pope Boniface IV for the Byzantine Emperor Phocas' gift of the Pantheon, which was dedicated by him to the Virgin and all the Martyrs. The Byzantine exarch, Smaragdus, placed a gilt bronze statue of the Emperor on its summit, and a long and high-flown inscription on the base.

The fine Corinthian column, with its fluted shaft of white marble, is a good piece of work of the best Imperial times, and we must therefore suppose that it was taken from some earlier building in the Forum or near by.

The actual **pavement of the Forum** is of great interest, especially the portion between Trajan's reliefs and the column of Phocas. Near the reliefs (at n. 15) can be seen traces of a small square space, once enclosed by a marble moulding, while the area inside is unpaved. Here stood the statue of Marsyas and the three historic trees — the fig, the olive, and the vine.

To the south of these monuments the pavement of the Forum is interrupted by a different kind of pavement that probably dates from the last years of the Republic. It is irregularly polygonal in shape and the travertine slabs show traces of altars or marble bases. This is the site of the **Lacus Curtius** (25), a kind of pond existing in Republican times as a memoria of the ancient marsh that once used to occupy the whole of the Forum valley. This pond was later entirely drained off, and only a welhead was left to recall its memory. Tradition relates that during the earliest years of the Republic, a noble Sabine, Mettius Curtius, flung himself on horseback into the chasm, in order to offer his life as a sacrifice for the State's welfare. This legend was much used by artists and it is shown on a relief in the *Nuovo Museo dei Conservatori* which has on the back an inscription of the same L. Naevius Surdinus, whom we have already mentioned.

On the SE the area of the Forum is limited by two bases of equestrian statues, (one dedicated to Domitian and the other to Constantine), and a large rectangular enclosure of brickwork, of early mediaeval date and of uncertain purpose.

Of the base of the **Equus Constantini** (27) there remains a portion of the central core of brick, originally covered with slabs of marble. The only trace of the **Equus Domitiani** (26), which was of colossal size, is the empty space in the pavement of the Forum left by the destruction of the upper part of the base, which was built of stone blocks. This rectangular base filled a considerable space between the *Equus Constantini* and the *Lacus Curtius* and rested on a massive concrete foundation that is still visible and in which are embedded three large travertine blocks that supported the three feet of the horse, by means of thick metal bars that went right through the base. Another travertine block was found at a lower level, with a cavity in which were found four vases of Latial type, of the 8th or 7th centuries B. C., very similar to those found in the archaic necropolis (44) of the Forum and of the Alban Hills.

7. – THE VICUS TUSCUS.

At the other end of the *Ima Sacra Via*, facing the Forum, we find ruins of the **Templum Divi Julii** (28), built in honor of Julius Caesar on the very spot where his body, pierced by 23 stabs in the Curia of Pompey's theatre, had been cremated on an improvised pyre. The ashes, placed in a precious urn, were deposited in the Mausoleum of the Julian *Gens* in the Campus Martius.

The building in the Forum (fig. 11) dedicated to the cult of the divine dictator was a small temple with a front of six Ionic columns. Before it stood a round altar, perhaps the original one, in a semicircular niche, which marked the actual spot where the body had been burnt. It is the only part of the building that is well preserved. On either side of this nich ewas a lofty base decorated with *rostra*, in memory of Caesar's plan of moving here the *Rostra* that stood on the other side of the Forum. The side that was on the Via Sacra was also decorated with a portico, whose marble fragments, together with those of the front, can be seen collected inside the foundations of the *cella* which have been emptied and lack their original filling. They are all of severe and early workmanship.

Soon after Caesar's murder an altar with the inscription *Parenti Patriae* and a column of Numidian marble 20 feet high were raised to his memory and were an object of continual strife.

Fig. 11. – Reconstruction of the Temple of Divus Julius.

Owing to the rivalary which arose about the person and the succession of *Divus Julius*, the Temple, which had been vowed in 42 B. C. by the triumvirs Mark Antony, Octavian, and Lepidus, was only dedicated by Augustus on the 10th of August 29 B. C.

Between the Temple of Caesar and the Temple of Castor stood the **Arch of Augustus** (29), spanning a minor branch of the Sacred Way. It had three passageways and was set up in his honor by the Senate and people of Rome in memory of the victory over Antony and Cleopatra in Actium (31 B. C.). Other people, however, are of the opinion that the arch was erected in 19 B. C., still in honor of Augustus, after the recovery of the banners taken from Crassus by the Parthians, and must have borne the *Fasti Consolari* e *Trionfali* on the inner walls of the side openings. The travertine foundations of the Arch where discovered in 1888, together with some doric fragments of the entablature. Some other fragments of the marble coating of the base had been known before and the dedicatory inscription on the attic had been copied in 1546.

Next to the right passage of the Arch started the stairway of the **Temple of Castor** (30), one of the few buildings in the Forum that has some portion of its entablature still *in situ*. The claracteristic and picturesque appearance of its ruins has in all ages attracted the attention of artists.

The foundation of the Temple is connected with one of the most popular legends of Roman history. At the battle of lake Regillus between the Etruscans with their Latin allies, and the Romans (496 B. C.), just as the battle began to turn favorably for the Roman arms, two youths were seen to withdraw from the fight. At the same moment two youths of divine appearance were seen watering their horses at the fountain of Juturna in the

Forum. The two Dioscuri, Castor and Pollux, had helped the Romans in the battle and had at once carried the news of victory to Rome.

As an offering of thanks for their succour, the dictator Postumius vowed them a Temple near that fountain of Juturna, which was afterward dedicated by his son in 484 B. C. Of this early Temple, rebuilt in 117 B. C. by Metellus in small blocks of tufa, some remains may be seen inside the great concrete substructure that dates from the time of Tiberius (6 A. D.). To the latter Emperor must also be attributed the three magnificent columns on the side. On the front are still to be seen, between the intercolumniations of the Imperial age, some of the column bases of the Temple of Metellus. Although dedicated to both the Dioscuri, Castor and Pollux, the name of the latter is never mentioned and the Temple is always known as that of Castor of the Castors.

The Temple is separated from the Basilica Julia by the **Vicus Tuscus,** the street that went from the Forum to the region of the Circus Maximus. The name is evidently derived from some neighboring quarter inhabited by Etruscans, and indeed tradition states that Tarquin the Proud gave the region of the *Vicus Tuscus* over to the Etruscan artists who were at work on the Temple of Jupiter Capitolinus.

On the left of the *Vicus Tuscus* stand two important buildings: the so called *Templum Augusti*, and the *Horrea Agrippiana*.

The so called **Temple of Augustus** derives its name from a temple that Livia, his wife, and Tiberius, his successor, erected to the founder of the Empire in the neighborhood of the Roman Forum. In reality, it is not a temple, but a wide monumental Vestibule built by Domitian for entrance to the Imperial buildings on the Palatine. The front overlooking the *Vicus Tuscus* consisted of a portico in strong brick pilasters coated with marble, through which the wide rectangular hall was entered. It was furnished with niches to contain statues and surmounted by a large vault. The portico continued on the shorter side facing the Temple of the Castors, ornamented with semicolumns and arches. The true temple of Augustus was probably situated near the Church of Santa Maria della Consolazione.

This building forms a part of the great general reconstruction of the Palatine, undertaken by Domitian, but only completed by his successors. The name of *Caius*, the Emperor Caligula, refers to an earlier building that formed the start of Caligula's famous **bridge** by means of which the Emperor was able to go from his palace on the Palatine to the Capitol without having to descend into the Forum. This bridge was simply a series of gangways, largely wooden, that connected the roofs of the various intervening buildings, among which the chief was the Basilica Julia. This bridge cannot have lasted long since it must have perished either during the fire of Nero, or the one that took place under Titus.

The other building is a great corn-market, probably built by Agrippa, as is proved by the name of **Horrea Agrippiana** (32), and by its construction in tufa *opus quadratum*.

The ancient marble plan of Rome shows that originally this market consisted of three large court yards, with large wooden roofs supported by brick pillars, and surrounded by two stories of rooms that served as store-rooms or shops. In later times, perhaps mediaeval, a number of houses were built on the site of these court-yards, thus entirely altering their appearance. In the center stands the shrine with the altar of the tutelary divinities of the *horrea*, easily distinguished from the mediaeval buildings by the modern roof and the fineness of its brickwork. A fountain stands before it. Architectural fragments of the travertine portico that fronted the *Vicus Tuscus* lie scattered about the area, as do also portions of the roofing of the inner rooms.

Returning to the back of the Temple of Castor we enter the **Church of S. Maria Antiqua** (Plan 33 and fig. 12). It was built above an earlier building of the time of Caligula, the *impluvium* of which is still visible at a lower level. The longer sides face north-east, very much the same orientation as the *Horrea* we have just examined, and may perhaps be the original *Atrium Gai*. Moreover the church is itself established inside an important and unusual Roman building, which it has hardly altered at all. The plan, while it agrees more or less with the general type

Fig. 12. — The so-called Temple of Augustus.
The central covered room with mediaeval pictures.

of the Christian basilicas, is on the other hand most remarkable for a pagan building. The construction points
to the time of Domitian. A number of authorities have
thought that it might be the library of the Temple of Augustus, but the comparison with those that have been identified with certainty in the Villa of Hadrian, in the Baths of
Caracalla, and on the Palatine, not to mention the ones
far from Rome, shows that it cannot have been a library.

The hypothesis that it was the *Atrium Minervae* does
not appear to be very admissible because the said *Atrium*
connected with the Temple of Augustus, which, as we
have already pointed out, is to be found elsewhere. We
should rather assume it to be the Guard-House or " prae-
torium " to which the surveillance of access to the Palatine was entrusted.

Next to the left aisle of the church is a wide corridor
which, as we already mentioned in discussing these buildings, leads up to the Palatine. It now consists of an incli-
ned plane paved with *opus spicatum*, portions of which are
still visible, and is divided into three ramps. Most of the
vaults are a restoration.

Although Christian monuments lie outside our scope
strictly speaking, we will, nevertheless, glance at the frescoes that decorate the Church. The founders of the parish of *S. Maria Antiqua* chose the building because its
plan agreed very closely with the ordinary type of church
of that period. Later, after the first decoration in fresco,
an apse was cut in the rear wall.

A square atrium stood in front of the church, which was itself divided into three naves with small chapels at the end of the aisles. The Christian additions, besides the apse, were the presbiterium, the *schola cantorum* and the narthex in front of the entrance.

The frescoes have been much discussed, and belong to four different epochs, not all of which can be defined with any certainty. Those of the upper and therefore most recent layer, with the figures of various Saints and persons whose names are given in Greek inscriptions, bear also the figures of Popes St. Zacharias (741-752), St. Stephen II (752-757), and St. Paul I (757-767). The lower layers are at least a century earlier and lead us to date the foundation of the church at about the beginning of the 7th century A. D. The second layer can indeed be dated at 649 A. D. The most interesting pictures are those of the left aisle, with Christ enthroned in the center with various saints on either side, and scenes of the Old Testament above. Also interesting are those of the neighboring chapel with the scene of the Crucifixion (fig. 13) and others on the walls with the story of St. Julitta and her son St. Quiricus. In the apse was the figure of Christ with the Virgin and Pope St. Paul I. Other paintings are to be seen on the wall of the *schola cantorum* (to the right Isaiah and Hezekiah, David and Goliath) and on the columns.

The church was abandoned under Leo IV (845-856) after a severe earthquake, since it was always threatened with landslips from the ruined Palatine. The parish was transferred to S. Maria Nova, now known as S. Francesca Romana.

Fig. 13. — Fresco in S. Maria Antiqua. The Crucifixion.

To the left of the entrance to S. Maria Antiqua there is a large room with an apse in the center, usually closed by a wooden fence. This is the **Oratory of the Forty Martyrs** (34), dedicated to the memory of the forty soldiers who during the persecution of Diocletian, were martyred in Armenia by being frozen to death in a large tank. The apse is decorated with the scene of the martyrdom. The decoration of the walls should also be noticed, especially the two crosses on the left with medallions in the center and crowns and various ornaments hanging from the arms.

8. – THE MONUMENTS OF VESTA.

While going from the Oratory of the Forty Martyrs towards the Arch of Augustus, we cross an important group of monuments which, according to tradition, are among the oldest in the whole Forum. The first is the **Spring of Juturna** (35) which is composed of a square marble-lined basin; a shrine originally holding the image of the goddess, protectress of the waters; and a marble wellhead, placed there by the Aedilis M. Barbatius Pollio under Augustus. The monument has been recently restored with pieces of the original architecture. On the edge of the **Lucus Juturnae** (36) stands a pretty marble altar found in the near neighborhood. On the front and back there are reliefs representing the two Dioscuri and their sister Helen, who is represented as the goddess of light, while on the shorter sides are their parents, Jupiter and Leda. The cult of the two Dioscuri, Castor and Pollux, was connected with that of Juturna, since here, at her spring, they are said to have watered their horses after the battle of Lake Regillus.

In antiquity these medicinal waters were eagerly sought after by the sick, and rooms were built behind the pool for the use of visitors. Here are kept all the different fragments of sculpture that were found in the excavation of the sanctuary: notably a statue of Apollo, copy of an original of the 5th century B. C.; a statue of Aesculapius; and parts of two horses from a group of the Dioscuri that decorated the base in the middle of the pool.

To the east of the sanctuary of Juturna can be seen the remains of a round building. This is the famous **Temple of Vesta** (37) where the Vestal Virgins guarded the sacred fire, which, symbolic of the life of Rome, could never be allowed to go out. The Temple was often destroyed by fire, the last time under Commodus in 191 A. D., after which it was almost entirely rebuilt by Julia Domna, wife of Septimius Severus. To this reconstruction must also be attributed the ruins still existing (fig. 14). The building was surrounded by an elegant colonnade of Corinthian style, closed by fine grilles, and was raised on a short flight of steps above the level of the Forum. There is a good representation of the Temple on an ancient relief in the Uffizi Museum in Florence, although it is earlier than the reconstruction of Severus and even perhaps than that of Nero. A section of the elegant building has been reconstructed by inserting

Fig. 14. – The Temple of Vesta. Partial reconstruction.

the original marble fragments in the modern travertine restoration.

Although considered to be almost contemporary with the foundation of Rome itself, it stood outside the area of *Roma Quadrata* and must therefore belong to a later development of the city, when the Forum valley had been drained. It had never been inaugurated or consecrated as a Temple and could not be used as a meeting-place by the Senate.

There was no image of the goddess inside the Temple itself. Therefore, the cult statue of Vesta was kept in a small shrine built against the wall of the House of the Vestal Virgins to the right of the entrance. It had two columns on the front and has been partially restored.

To the left are the steps that lead into the House of the Vestals or **Atrium Vestae** (38), as it was called in antiquity. This was the residence of the six priestesses of the goddess, who were held in the greatest honor by the Romans, since it was the only priesthood held exclusively by women. The vows were not taken for life, but usually for a period of thirty years, during which the Vestal was obliged to remain virgin, although enjoying considerable freedom. The Vestals alone, together with the Empress, had the right of going about the city in a chariot. They had a special boy at all the spectacles and a place of honour at the principal functions. The State gave each Vesta a large dowry, which she could spend as best she liked.

Fig. 15. — The peristyle of the House of the Vesta.

Their fine house (fig. 15) was restored, enlarged
and beautified (as may be seen by the different brickwork), by Nero, Domitian, Trajan, and by Septimius
Severus, who enlarged it on the southeast. It consists
of a central court or atrium surrounded by a portico
with two stories, the lower columns being of *cipollino*,
the upper of *breccia*. In the middle of the court
are three fountain-basins, restored in modern times.
The central one (fig. 16, *a*) is the oldest, and used
to be the impluvium of the early house which was
restored by Nero and still further by Domitian after the
great fire of 80 A. D. The chief living and reception
rooms are to be found in the two stories on the South
and West, while on the northern side was a row of shops
with a portico in front.

The wings of the courtyard are decorated with the
statues and honorary bases of some *Vestales Maximae*,
the heads of the order, who had deserved the gratitude
of the state " for their morals and chastity, and for their
exemplary care for the sacred functions. " Near the
entrance is a base on which the name of the Vestal to
whom it had been dedicated has been erased. It may
possibly have belonged to a certain Claudia, who, according to Prudentius, abandoned the cult of Vesta in order to
embrace Christianity. On account of such apostacy,
her name would certainly have been erased from all her
monuments. The dwelling-rooms run all around the
atrium. We may recognize the oven (*d*) near the south-

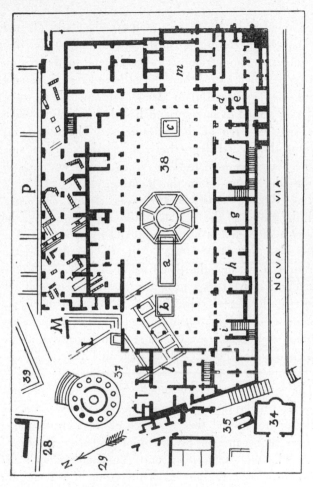

Fig. 16. – The plan of the House of the Vestals.

ern corner of the house, the mill (e); the baths (f); the kitchen (g); the *lararium*, or private chapel (i); and the *triclinium*, or dining room (l). At the end of the atrium is a room much larger than the others, which is usually called the *tablinum* (m) or drawing-room. It is more probably a kind of sacristy and has three rooms on each side, one for each of the priestesses. The bed-rooms were on the second floor, that rose on the southern side of the house towards the *Via Nova*, the street that still divides the Forum from the Palatine.

The **Regia Pontificis** (39) was closely connected with the House of the Vestals. Here tradition placed the residence of Numa in his double capacity as King and as founder of the cult of Vesta. After the expulsion of the Tarquins it became the dwelling of the *rex sacrificulus*. The Pontifex Maximus probably dwelt in a part of the House of the Vestals, the *Domus Publica*, and the Regia became a small symbolical building, for its plan is absolutely unsuitable for a dwelling. This was the official residence of the Pontifex Maximus and had to be near the Temple of Vesta.

The building was very small. Since under the Empire the Emperors assumed all the sacerdotal power as well and transferred the residence of the Pontiff to the Palatine, it became simply a formal and traditional edifice. The real Republican and Augustan walls of the *Regia* can justbe recognized at the ground level, and are unfortunately covered with unchecked vegetation. Several wells of considerable antiquity are to be seen inside the area. They had perhaps a ritual significance.

The various fragments of the architectural decoration that are scattered about the neighborhood belong to the second reconstruction in 36 B. C. by Domitius Calvinus, and are very similar to those of the Temple of Caesar. The *Clivus Vestae* ran between the *Regia* and the House of the Vestals.

9. – THE MEDIA VIA SACRA.

The ruins which extend to the right of the Media Sacra Via, between the Regia and the Arch of Titus, have been placed in an entirely new light through the researches of Dr. Esther B. Van Deman (*American Journal of Archaeology*, 1924). Prof. Lanciani had already noticed in this confused mass of ruins the traces of the piers of an immense **Porticus** (Plan 41) built of large blocks of travertine. Most of these blocks had been taken away during the destruction of the building, but their position was fixed by the later Imperial concrete wall that had been built to close the arcades. Basing his hypothesis on some inscriptions which mentioned the *margaritarii de Sacra via*, Prof. Lanciani suggested that this portico might have been used by the merchants who dealt in pearls and other jewellery of eastern origin.

However the recent studies have shown that this portico is much older and vaster. These same tra vertine piers are to be found on the other side of the Sacred Way, even under the Basilica of Constantine, and reach almost to the *Regia* and the Temple of Romulus. The only building with which this gigantic portico can be associated is the Golden House of Nero, which certainly extended to the Forum. This may well be the portico that formed the Vestibule of that vast palace. Therefore the blocks from a travertine arch that lie on either side of the *Via Sacra* must be attributed to this portico and not to the *Fornix Fabianus*, a triumphal arch raised in 121 B. C. by Q. Fabius Maximus in remembrance of his own victory over the Allobroges, of that of Aemilius Paullus over the Macedonians, and of that of Scipio Africanus over the Carthaginians. The exact position of this arch is still unknown. The enormous concrete cores of walls that lie scattered all over this area, especially in front of the Basilica of Constantine, and that were hitherto considered to be of late Imperial times, belong to the foundations of this portico.

Here also are to be seen the marble remains of a small round **Temple of Bacchus** (42), perhaps a simple shrine, that was restored, according to the fragmentary inscription, by Antoninus Pius, together with a Temple of Cybele that stood between the Forum and the Palatine.

On the other side of the Via Sacra, opposite the *Regia* stands the fine **Temple of Antoninus and Faustina** (43), raised on a right platform and approached by a staircase which has been restored in modern times. The portico, composed of six columns of *cipollino*, with a richly sculptured frieze, is one of the finest ruins in the Forum and one of the most perfect architectural remains of the Roman world.

The inscription on the architrave shows that in was at first dedicated to Faustina alone, and later, by a decree of the Senate (*ex senatus consulto*), to Antoninus Pius after his death in 161 A. D. The well-preserved side walls are of regular peperino masonry and were faced with slabs of marble framed by pilasters. Today inside the Temple is the Church of St. Lorenzo in Miranda. In the Portico are fragments of two colossal statues — one male the other female. They were discovered at the foot of the Temple and are perhaps the images of the Imperial couple.

To the south-east of the Temple can be seen a small free space covered with a modern pavement, on which are traced, in plots of grass, the outlines of some circular and rectangular tombs. To the extreme right, under cover, is a pit with some of the original graves at the bottom. It is the only part of the **Archaic Cemetery** (44), discovered in 1902, that could be preserved. The tombs belong to the iron age between the 9th and 7th century B. C., and are of two classes. The older are the cremation burials, with the ashes collected in a cinerary urn (usually shaped like a hut), at the bottom of a pit, in some cases within a large jar to protect them. The inhumation

5

burials are later in date and have sometimes damaged the earlier pit-burials. The bodies were placed in a tufa or wooden coffin, or sometimes just placed on the ground. Both groups were found with the funerary furniture all complete, usually consisting of rough vases, shaped by hand without the use of the potter's wheel, some few vases of black *bucchero*, and various bronze ornaments, especially *fibulae* and weapons.

The Sacred Way begins to rise from this point, and thus the poets often call this section of the road the *Clivus Sacer*. On either side of the road are numerous private buildings. To the left are some rooms belonging to a Republican *hospitium* (O). To the right are some more houses of the 2nd and 3rd centuries of the Empire (P), also built on the foundations of Republican houses and of the great portico of Nero's Golden House. Further on, to the left, is the so-called **Temple of the Divus Romulus** (45), dedicated to Romulus, the young son of Maxentius who died in 307 A. D. The plan of this small building is somewhat unusual. Instead of a rectangular *cella* surrounded by columns, it consists of a rotunda flanked on each side by rectangular rooms which end in semicircular apses and have on the front two elegant porticos (fig. 17). The original bronze door miraculously escaped the depredations of the barbarians. The working of the lock is of special interest. The interior of the building is now completely bare and is entered from the Church of SS. Cosma and Damiano to which it served

Fig. 17. – The so-called Temple of Divus Romulus.

as a vestibule up to a short time ago. Its entrance was at the level of the Via Sacra in the time of Maxentius, since the road had been raised by Nero.

The back of the Temple of Romulus is connected to a big building the walls of which consist of stone blocks, carefully squared, up to the height of more than fifteen meters. Towards the middle of the wall a door with jambs is visible, coated with travertine, which led into a rectangular hall ornamented with niches. It belonged to the *Forum Pacis* (Forum of the Peace) built by Vespasian after his victory over the Jews and the seizure of Jerusalem (70 A. D.). Inside the ancient hall is now the Church of SS. Cosma and Damiano where interesting mosaic-work of the 6th century A. D. can be seen.

Going now to the back of the building we can see the end wall which Septimius Severus restored in brickwork and on which he fixed his marble plan of the city (*Forma Urbis*) whose fragments were found near here and are now kept in the Conservatory Palace. Here we can also see the beautiful pavement of coloured marbles belonging to the Forum of Peace, as well as an enormous mass of concrete fallen from the top of the Basilica of Constantine.

Returning to the *Clivus Sacer* we pass in front of a small brick portico, near the western corner of the Basilica of Costantine, that belonged to a mediaeval house, which perhaps extended to the other side of the road, where there is a piece of wall shaped like an apse (Q).

10. – THE VELIA.

We now enter the **Basilica of Constantine** (47). It is said that this wonderful building, one of the most imposing constructions of the ancient world, inspired Michelangelo in the building of Saint Peter's, especially for the enormous piers that support the dome. It as also called the Basilica of Maxentius since it was founded by that Emperor in about 308 A. D., and was only finished by Constantine after his victory over Maxentius at *Sacra Rubra* (313 A. D.). The present remains of the Basilica comprise all one side and a part of the principal apse on the shorter side toxards the Forum of Peace. The aisles were composed of three huge rooms covered with barred vaults, above which sprang the cross vaults that covered the central nave. In the original plan of Maxentius the orientation of the Basilica was according to its length, and the principal entrance was to have been on a side street at right angles to the Sacra Via (fig. 18).

Constantine altered the axis of the Basilica, and moved the main entrance on to the Sacred Way, where he built a portico as an approach, while opposite he built a new apse with a characteristic architectural decoration. There was a seated colossal statue of Constantine in the main apse and its fragments, discovered in 1490, are now in the courtyard of the Conservatory Palace. In front of the main piers stood eight gigantic columns of Proconnesian marble, the last of which was removed by Paul V and placed in front of the Church of S. Maria Maggiore.

The destruction of all the left aisle of the Basilica probably began under Pope Leo IV (845-857), when one of

Fig. 18. – Basilica of Constantine.

the most terrible earthquakes that has been recorded devastated the city. It was later carried on throughout all the Middle Ages, when the whole population used it as a quarry for their own buildings. We must be thankful that its wonderful solidity has withstood these attacks so well, a proof of the great architectural ability of the Romans even in the age of Constantine.

Fig. 19. – The Arch of Titus on the Summa Sacra Via.

Following the *Clivus Sacer* we reach the **Arch of Titus** (48), standing on the highest point of the Velia, that descends from here towards the Colosseum and the Suburra (fig. 19). It is a fitting memorial of the victory over the Jews and of the conquest and destruction of Jerusalem in 70 A. D. These events were celebrated by a triumph of such unusual magnificence that it was immortalized in the reliefs, on the arch, inside the archway, and on the outside frieze. The great pictorial reliefs on either side of the passageway represent the two principal mo-

Fig. 20. — Detail of the Arch of Titus.
The spoils of the Temple of Jerusalem.

ments of the triumph. To the left the Goddess Rome herself leads the four-horsed triumphal chariot into the city, while a victory descends from Heaven to crown the Emperor. On the right (fig. 20) is shown the procession carrying the spoils of the Temple of Jerusalem, including the seven-branched candlestick, the silver trumpets, and the table of the shewbread. In the center of the coffered ceiling is depicted the Apotheosis of Titus, who is carried up to heaven by an eagle. This relief and the inscription on the attic prove the Arch to have been built or finished after the death of Titus by his brother Domitian.

The sides of the Arch, which were destroyed in the Middle Ages when the Frangipani incorporated it in their fortifications, were accurately restored by Valadier in 1821. The modern work, in travertine, can be easily distinguished from the ancient, which is of marble throughout.

Recent excavations have revealed under the foundations of the Arch some earlier constructions, perhaps belonging to private houses.

The foundations of the arch overlap the *Clivus Sacer* of Augustus which had been replaced by the straight road of Nero, a part of which descended through it to the Colosseum valley. In front of the arch a branch road, the *Clivus Palatinus*, led through the *Porta Mugonia* to the Palatine and the Flavian Palace.

We have now to examine the *Nova via*, that is the road which runs at the foot of the Palatine, parallel to the *Via Sacra* and bounds the Roman Forum toxards the SW. It derives its name from having been constructed after the *Via Sacra* in order to furnish the buildings situated on the slopes of the Palatine with a means of communication. A number of remains of these buildings, such as shops, staircases and private houses, are still visible up to the summit of the hill. Some arches cross the road to strengthen the second story of the House of the Vestals overlooking the right side. The buildings erected by Domitian on the Northern corner of the Palatine caused the interruption of the *Nova Via*, once going down to the *Velabrum*. The *Nova Via* was replaced by a slope which, starting from the so-called Temple of Augustus, reached the *Clivus Victoriae*.

THE PALATINE

I. – HISTORICAL INTRODUCTION.

The Palatine hill rises to the east of the Tiber valley and has the shape of a large die with a trapezoidal surface. Its almost perpendicular slopes are crowned by a wide and pleasant plateau 168 ft. above sea level (at S. Bonaventura). The Palatine is not really either the loftiest or most spacious of the hills of Rome, but is the most isolated one of all, in a central position near the crossing of the Tiber, the natural line of communication of all the populations that lay along its banks.

In ancient times the hill did not form the solid, level block that it does to-day. Its present appearance is the result of the long and tireless labors of the Emperors. During the Republic and still more during the earliest times of Rome, it was divided into three distinct summits. The *Palatium* was the principal one and overlooked the Circus Maximus and the Caelian hill. Its highest point is where the Convent of S. Bonaventura now rises, and under the Empire was built upon especially by the Flavian Em-

perors. The second was the *Germalus*, on the side looking towards the Capitol and the Forum, now principally
occupied by the Farnese Gardens; lastly, towards the
valley of the Colosseum, was the Velia, on which stands
the Arch of Titus. The hollows that divided these three
summits have now been largely explored by the recent
excavations of Boni under the Palace of the Flavii and
near the so-called House of Caligula. The results of these
excavations have been very important since here have
been found the remains of the late Republican houses that
were afterwards used to support the Imperial buildings.

The Palatine was the cradle of Rome even as the Forum
was the heart of the city. Tradition relates that Romulus,
when he drew up the city's first constitution, divided the
population into three tribes, the *Ramnes*, the *Tities* and
the *Luceres*, the tribes that were supposed to have inhabited the three summits of the hill before it was united
into one. The union of all these various tribes into a single
city, with its own government and laws, is what we call the
foundation of Rome, and is placed by tradition in the 8th.
century (753 B. C.). Somewhat later the hill was surrounded with a strong wall of tufa blocks, and, since the
plan was that of a more or less regular rectangle, the city
thus fortified was called **Roma Quadrata.**

Such was the earliest Rome, the Rome of the Kings,
an age that is now coming to light again thanks to recent
excavations and a more rational system of historical criticism. It now appears a glorious period during which,

little by little, the city on the small hill subdued the inhabitants of the neighboring hills. Thus grew up first the city of the **Septimontium** formed by the union of the three summits of the Palatine (*Palatium, Germalus, Velia*) with the four summits of the Esquiline (*Oppius, Cispius, Fagutal, Subura*, the latter name probably being used originally to describe the height of the Caelian which is nearest to the Esquiline). Later came the **City of the Four Regions**, when to the original nucleus had been added the Quirinal with its dependencies, the Capitoline, the Viminal and the Caelian (the regions were: *Suburana*, that included the Caelian, *Esquilina*, *Palatina* and *Collina*, the latter also embracing the Quirinal). Lastly the whole city was surrounded by the formidable line of fortification known as the **Servian Walls.**

With the extension of the area of the city the Palatine lost its former importance, but it remained the center of the religious memories and rites of the city, and because of its delightful position gradually became the favorite residential quarter of the wealthier Romans. We know a few of these householders: *Q. Lutatius Catulus*, consul with Marius in 102 B. C. who together with him gained the famous victory at Vercelli over the Cimbrian invaders; *M. Livius Drusus*, tribune of the people in 19 B. C. who was assassinated by his political rival Q. Varius; *Crassus* the orator, who inherited the house of Drusus and richly restored it and renewed it, being the first person in Rome to employ columns of Hymettian marble, a fact which led

to its purchase in 62 B. C. by *Cicero* who paid L. 30,000
for it (it remained in existence till Caligula enclosed it
within his palace); *Publius Clodius*, the notorius tribune
and demagogue, slain by Milo on the Via Appia in 58 B.
C.; *M. Aemilius Scaurus*, the stepson of Sulla, whose house
was considered the finest of all, so much so that on his
death Clodius bought it at once for over L. 40,000 although
he had already spent L. 6,000 on his own; *Hortensius*,
the orator whose house was later bought and enlarged by
Augustus, as well as many other well-known individuals
of the last years of the Republic.

All these residences were on the slopes of the hill
overlooking the *Clivus Victoriae* and the Forum, that is to
say on the *Germalus*, and were destroyed or modified when
Tiberius and Caligula built their Palaces (fig. 21).

The surface of the Palatine was thus fully occupied
when, at the fall of the Republic, the Emperors selected
it for their residence. As it was the most fashionable
residential quarter of the city, it is clear that the Emperors
would whoose to dwell there, and they came into possession of the property of former owners by means not always
scrupulously honest.

Augustus began by simply enlarging the house of Hortensius (Plan n. 10), and regularly expropriated all the
area ceeded for his new buildings such as the Temple of
Vesta (11), the Temple of Apollo Palatinus (12), the Portico of the Danaids (14) and the Libraries (22). Tiberius
however, started the custom of covering the hill with im-

Fig. 21. – The Palatine seen from the Roman Forum.

mense buildings (15), more suitable for a royal residence
than the small and out-of-the-way house of Augustus.
These buildings rendered it necessary to demolish a great
number of constructions, and wrought great alterations
in the appearance of the hill itself. Tiberius chose the
Germalus summit, which was still in his time the most important section of the Palatine, and he was followed by
Caligula who extended the buildings still further north,
right up to the Forum (17), thus occupying all the Germalus.

These were part of Nero's Domus Transitoria and
were burned in the great fire of 64 A. D. Nero then built
over their ruins the great foundations which still remain
to support the Golden House and, in order to link it with
the various buildings on the Palatine, he built the fine
cryptoporticus (19 and 19-*a*) that runs as far as the house
of Augustus.

Domitian is the great rebuilder of the Palatine and
of a large portion of the city itself as well. Since he found
two of the summits of the hill already covered, he turned
his attention to the third, still free but of very uneven
surface. By means of colossal works he was able to trans-
form it into a sumptuous residence, which Martial (*Epig.*,
VII, 56) called worthy of the Gods (*Parrhasia*). The little
valley that lay between the *Velia* and the *Palatium* was
filled with the debris of the *Domus Transitoria* itself, and
an artificial platform was thus formed on which were
built the various rooms of the Flavian Palace.

But the vast plans of Domitian and of his architect Rabirius did not cease here. It was therefore necessary to build a second Palace to the south of the first (23) as the real residence of the Emperor, while the first remained the official Palace, in which all the great court functions took place, very much in the same way as Buckingham Palace and St. James's. And still further to the south was built the magnificent stadium, perhaps better called hippodrome (24), for gymnastic exercises and for the idle sauntering of the court. On the corner of the hill towards the Caelian the building of a complete therma establishment was begun, and for this purpose it was necessary to build great foundations and supporting walls.

Both the second Palace, usually called the *Domus Augustana*, and the hippodrome were continued by Trajan; the Baths were only finished about a century later under Septimius Severus. Hadrian built the great substructures over the *Clivus Victoriae*, with the object of increasing the area of the *Domus Tiberiana*, extending out as far as the Forum with a front on the *Via Nova* (16). These arches were afterwards strengthened by Septimius Severus.

After Hadrian there was not much building activity on the Palatine till the time of Septimius Severus. Great bathing establishments had by that time become fashionable; the Palatine did not have any nor was there any vacant space on which they could be built. Septimius

6

Severus therefore continued the colossal plan of Domitian.
By means of a series of arcades from 20 to 30 metres high,
he increased the area of the hill to the south, right up to
the steps of the Circus Maximus (fig. 22) and built his
Baths on top (26). He connected them with the back
of Domitian's handsome box on the Hippodrome (25),
and built another, still finer, overlooking the Circus
Maximus (28), from which he could assist at the games
held thirty metres below, and with the whole Circus, full
of 250 thousand persons, lying at his feet. Lastly, at the
most southern corner of the hill he built his famous
Septizonium, one of the best known landmarks of Rome
till the close of the 16th century.

After Septimius Severus no important works were
executed on the Palatine which was by this time congested
with buildings. Diocletian and Constantine abandoned
the Palatine and built themselves more modern residences
elsewhere both in Rome and in the more distant parts of
the Empire. Thus began the rapid decline of the hill
which was hastened by the abandonment of the ancient
sanctuaries.

* * *

The history of the hill during the Middle Ages is
plunged in almost totale obscurity. An inscription of the
Emperors Valens, Valentinian and Gratian, that was copied
by the anonymous pilgrim of Einsiedeln *in foro Palatini*
(the *area Palatina*) in the eighth century, mentions some
restorations to the buildings of the hill. We know that

Fig. 22. — The Palatine seen from the Aventine (Du Pérac, 16th century).

the barbarian Kings who invaded Rome during the 5th and 6th centuries, especially Odoacer and Theodoric, took up their residence in the old Palace of the Caesars, as a tangible sign of their power. Heraclius in 629 A. D. was solemnly received on the Palatine by the Senate, assembled in the great throne room (21, *B*). Strictly speaking the buildings were the property of the Emperors of the East, the rightful heirs of the Western Empire, and they kept a representative there, but the Popes had already occupied some areas here and there, dedicating some as churches and giving others to monasteries.

The earliest Christian remain of the Palatine is the little **Chapel of S. Caesarius** (23), which was dedicated on the spot where the *lararium* of the Imperial Palace had been, and was destined to be a real "palatine chapel." Next to it in the 9th century was built a **Greek Monastery** that rose to great importance especially during the 12th cent. when Eugenius III was elected here in 1145. Both these buildings were afterwards incorporated in the fortifications of the Frangipani which occupied the whole of the *Velia* and a considerable portion of the *Palatium*.

The more the authority of the Eastern Emperors decreased, especially after the defeats of the Greek armies during the Gothic invasions, the more the power of the Popes increased. Inside the templum Heliogabali (the present *Vigna Barberini*), a **Church** was dedicated to **St. Sebastian** (38), who, according to his Acts, had suffered martyrdom in the hippodrome of the *Palatium*, as the

whole Palatine hill was called throughout the Middle
Ages. The neighboring Abbey of St. Gregory in the mean-
while obtained possession of the Septizonium, and shortly
afterwards of the Baths of Severus (29), also called the
minor Septizonium.

The Palatine is also connected with another famous
monastery, which belonged to the Benedictines of Montecassino, and was called *in Pallara* from its position on the
eastern side of the hill. During the 14th cent. it became
for some time the seat of the Abbot of Montecassino himself.

From that time to the 14th cent. the records are silent;
during the Renaissance the hill is described as the *Palazzo
Maggiore*. About 1550 Cardinal Alessandro Farnese,
nephew of Paul III, bought nearly the whole of the Germalus, where he laid out the gardens that are still one of
the delights of the hill, and built the pavilion now occupied
by the Director of the excavations.

During the whole of the 16th and still more during
the 17th cent., the Palatine was the scene of a series of
irregular excavations due especially to the Farnese. They
still further devastated the ancient buildings and hastened
their complete ruin. During the following century the
first systematic excavations were begun, at first under
the direction of Bianchini (fig. 23), then under that of the
abbé Rancoureuil, and later, at the beginning of the 19th
century on the part of the Napoleonic prefect de Tournon.
In 1860 Napoleon III bought the Farnese Gardens from

Fig. 23. — Relief with a sacrifice scene found during the excavations of Bianchini.

the Bourbons of Naples and gave the direction of the excavations to the able architect Pietro Rosa. In 1870 the property passed into the hands of the Italian Government, and formed the nucleus of the public property on the Palatine. Shortly afterwards were added the possessions of the suppressed convents of St. Bonaventura and of the Visitation (Villa Mills), and finally that of the Barberini, so that now the whole hill is public property.

2. – THE CORNER TOWARDS THE VELABRUM.

There are two ways of access to the Palatine: one on the Via dei Fori Imperiali together with the Roman Forum and one on the Via di S. Gregorio (already Via dei Trionfi), half way between the Arch of Constantine and the Piazzale del Circo Massimo.

Those who enter from the Via dei Fori go through the Via Sacra to the Arch of Titus, and from here to the Clivus Palatinus which leads directly to the Flavian Palace and the House of Livia. If one wishes to visit everything, at the Arch of Titus one must take the Via Nova which runs round the foot of the Palatine, between this and the Roman Forum (see the map of the Forum 10). It joins the Clivus Victoriae below the Domus Tiberiana (n. 1), and the west end of the Cermalus (ns. 2-5), then go up on a modern path through the Area Palatina (n. 11), and the Temple of Apollo (n. 12). Alternatively one can go to the Clivus Victoriae and once there can enter the Criptoporti-

cus of Nero, through substructures of the Casino Farnese (ns. 17-18). The Criptoporticus will take one straight to the Cermalus which is the earliest hill of Rome, where are found the most ancient monuments (ns. 5-9).

Visitors who enter by the Via di S. Gregorio can go straight to the Stadium of Domitian (ns. 3 and 34), proceeding from there to the Domus Augustana (n. 23) and the Domus Flaviorum (n. 23). This way does not follow the chronological sequence of the Palatine. We suggest therefore that visitors go through the modern tunnel connecting the aforesaid entrance to the Arch of Titus, and from the arch pass by the building, n. 17, taking the Criptoporticus of Nero (n. 19) up to the Cermalus (D-E).

If there is only time for a short visit, instead of taking the following route which circles the hill from the Arch of Titus around towards the East and South by the Clivus Victoriae and the Velabro, it would be advisable to go straight up by the Clivus Palatinus, and so, skirting the Orti Farnesiani, come immediately to the House of Livia and the Templus Magnae Matris. In this case the study of the monuments will begin at the Scalae Caci (5).

The **Clivus Victoriae** was the principal road which gave access to the hill in antiquity and which started from the Velabrum. It got its name from an ancient sanctuary, the **Temple of Victory,** which was older, according to tradition, than the city itself, having been founded by Evander near the Porta Romanula of Roma Quadrata. We know nothing definite about this Temple which was rebuilt in 293 B. C. by Consul Lucius Postumius, and later by Caligula, after whom it was called *Victoria Germaniciana*. We do not know where it stood. It is mentioned in two inscriptions found near S. Teodoro, and the name *Clivus Victoriae* given to the road that went up this side of the hill leads one to suppose that it was somewhere in this neighborhood. Near the western corner are the remains of the fort fications of the hill, belonging to the time of **Roma Quadrata** (2). The walls are built with somewhat small but carefully cut blocks of light grey tufa, rich in carbonized fragments, that come from the quarries of the city of Fidenae (fig. 24).

Behind this section of wall there is an ancient *pozzolana* quarry, which was afterwards coated with stucco, and used as a cistern (fig. 25, 2). A well was dug down to it from above. The walls go right around the corner and may be seen to continue along the other side, where they are hidden by later buildings.

Roma Quadrata, as was mentioned in the historical introduction, is the city of the time of the Kings. When the city increased and spread far beyond the limits of the Palatine hill, the memory of this earliest settlement was kept by an altar named for it and built of squared masonry, which stood over a circular pit, the **Mundus.** This pit was supposed to represent the ideal center of the hill, the intersection of the *cardo* and the *decumanus*. Into it each year were thrown the first fruits of the harvest, while every stranger who wished to be admitted into the city threw

Fig. 24. – Walls of the city of Roma Quadrata.

a handful of earth of his native country into it. In front of this altar there was a large open space called the *Area Palatina*, next to the Temple of the Apollo and the house of Augustus.

The system of fortification of *Roma Quadrata* is perfect and shows that the builders were very expert and technically advanced. The wall, which the ancients called the *Murus Romuli*, was built half way up the hillside, and not on the summit, in order to add to its solidity and at the same time increase the area above. The blocks are dovetailed together and their thickness decreases towards the top. At the foot of the hill there must have been a ditch as an extra defense. There seem to have been only three gates: the *Porta Romanula* (fig. 25, 1) that stood at the point where the *Clivus Victoriae* passes under the Hadrianic arches; the gate on the *Scalae Caci*, which we will shortly describe; and the *Porta Mugonia*, opposite the principal entrance to the Flavian Palace, between the *Palatium* and the *Velia*.

The **Lupercal,** is the ancient cave of Faunus Lupercus who lived, according to the legends, in this corner of the hill before the foundation of the city; all the ancient writers place it opposite the Velabrum. The cave was venerated right up to the latest times of the Empire, and was surrounded by a thick grove, while a spring of fresh water rose in the interior. Before is stood the *ficus ruminalis*, under which the chest bearing the infants Romulus and Remus was supposed to have been washed ashore.

A special entrance connected the Lupercal with the Circus Maximus, and inside the sanctuary stood the famous group of the wolf suckling the twins, as a memorial of their preservation. This group appears on the earliest coins of Rome, but must not be confused with the well-known one now in the Conservatory Palace, which is an Etruscan work of the first years of the 5th century B. C. The figures of the twins were only added during the Renaissance, while the attitude of the wolf is different from that which we see on the coins.

Following the contours of the hill, immediately after some vaulted rooms (fig. 25, 4) we come to a depression

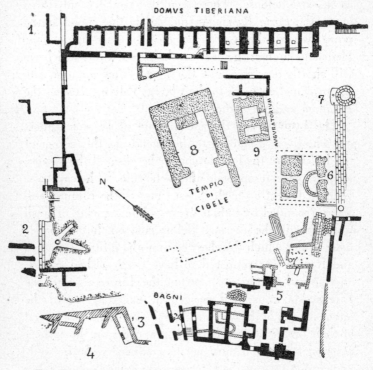

Fig. 25. – Plan of the area adjacent to the Temple of Cybele.

by which we can go up to the summit of the hill and to the *Area Palatina*. This depression in its upper portion follows an ancient road, the so-called **Scalae Caci** or the steps of Cacus, from the name of the famous thief who stole the oxen of Hercules. Here stood the second gate of *Roma Quadrata*, built at the end of a corridor, that turned sharply to the right at the top, so as to render its defense easier (fig. 25, 4-5-6).

The **Group of Buildings** (fig. 25, 5) standing to the north of the lower branch of the steps of Cacus, and excavated in 1907 by Vaglieri, are of very uncertain origin. Some portions appear to be connected with the fortifications of the so-called Romulean gateway, while others seem to be merely substructures of the hill founded on earlier buildings. We also think that here should be placed the *Casa Romuli*, perhaps identical with the *tugurium Faustuli*, that is to say, the hut on the heights of the Germalus in which Romulus and Remus were brought up, and which was remembered till quite late times.

Recently, an excavation job, executed between Caci Stairs and Magna Mater temple, (fig. 25, 5-8) has brought out some vestiges of *big huts* set on rocks. Such huts are of elliptical shape, turned all around with holes to insert wooden beams.

Near the fireplace has been found a great plenty of moulding belonging to the first and second iron age (eighth to fourth century B. C.), contemporary therefore to the foundation of Rome (754 B. C.). which fully confirms the historic tradition concerning the origin of Rome (fig. 25,3).

3. – THE " CERMALUS ".

In the present state of topographical knowledge it is
impossible to fix the exact position of the *Area Palatina*,
the central square of the hill where was the altar of the
Roma Quadrata, but it must be sought not far from the
Temple of Cybele (fig. 25, 8), from the house of Augustus (10), and from the Temple of Apollo (12). Here indeed are the most ancient buildings on the hill, including,
on the S E of the square, the remains (fig. 25, 6) of a concrete base, originally faced with stone masonry. Underneath it there is a large round building, whose walls are
made of large slabs of *capellaccio*, and which may possibly
be the **mundus,** the ritual pit of early Rome.

To the east of the *Roma Quadrata* is a **circular pit,**
also very ancient, built of small blocks of tufa that could
be carried by hand, and with a beehive or corbelled vault,
like the Greek *tholoi*, with rings gradually decreasing in
diameter, till it could be covered with one central slab
(fig. 25, 7). It is lined with stucco and behind is a wellhead which drew the water of the main cistern, after it
had been filtered by passing through a layer of sand and
other porous material.

We now pass to the **Templum Magnae Matris** (8),
one of the oldest buildings on the Palatine, on the top of
which grows a picturesque grove of ilexes. The Temple
is built according to the classic plan of the *megaron*, that

Fig. 26. – The Temple of Magna Mater on a relief
in the Villa Medici.

is to say with a rectangular *cella*, with the side walls prolonged so as to form two *antae*. In front there was an ample staircase and the Temple itself was raised on a lofty podium, according to the Roman custom requiring the sanctuaries to be removed from contact with the earth. This podium is built of concrete and was externally covered with blocks of *peperino*. Of the same stone, coated with stucco, were made the other architectural portions of the Temple. It was founded in 204 B. C.; was restored the first time by Metellus, consul in 110 B. C.; and was finally rebuilt by Augustus in 3 B. C., as he himself mentions in his will. Inside was kept the silver image of Cybele, the Great Mother of the Gods. In place of the head it had a conical stone, fallen from heaven. The Romans, obeying the instructions of Sybilline books, had brought this meteorite, supposed to be the symbol of the goddess, from Pessinus in Asia Minor during the Second Punic War (206 B. C.). After Augustus the Temple underwent no further restoration. The present podium is of the time of Metellus, and the architectural fragments of very severe style are probably of the 2nd century B. C. Augustus, in restoring it after the fire, simply gave the columns a new coating of stucco. It is probably depicted on a relief in the Villa Medici, formerly attributed to the *Ara Pacis* (fig. 26).

Cybele was supposed at first to be the mother of crops and sowings, personifying the creative force of nature, and therefore she came to be considered the Mother of the

Gods themselves. The attribution of the Temple to this Divinity is strengthened by the discovery, in 1872, of a headless statue of the Goddess, which was found near the pronaos of the Temple and is now kept near by.

Near the Temple of the Great Mother, there stands a smaller Temple of much later date, perhaps of the time of Hadrian. It is oriented on the same lines as the larger one, and is composed of two rooms. According to a recent theory it should be identified with the **Auguratorium** (fig. 25, 9), the spot whence the augurs, facing south, observed the flight of the birds before any important event.

The rooms behind the two Temples we have mentioned are a work of the Antonines, who placed them in front of the House of Tiberius (15, E). They were perhaps used as guard-rooms for the soldiers who were on duty at the palace. To the east of the Temples is the so-called *House of Livia*, which may now be definitely called the **House of Augustus,** the first Imperial residence on the Palatine.

The name of Livia was given to it from some lead water-pipes, inscribed with the name of *Julia*, that were found inside the house and are now on the wall of the *tablinum*. It has also been supposed to have been the paternal house of Tiberius, which later passed to Germanicus, but the latest researches enable us to attribute it with far greater probability to Augustus. Ovid (*Fast*. IV, 951) says that it stood near the Temples of Apollo and Vesta,

7

for Augustus had divided his property into three parts; one for Apollo one for Vesta, and one for himself. This house forms, as it were, the centre hall of the later Palaces which are connected with it by means of long passages, both open and covered. Although small by comparison with the great later Palaces, as a private residence it is by no means small, and the decorations show a high degree of taste on the part of the owner. Svetonius (*Augustus*, 72) mentions that Augustus lived in a small house, in no way remarkable either for size or ornament, with rooms without any marble of fine paving. From his description it is clear that the house was in existence in his day, and that it was kept as a kind of museum, since he mentions having seen some of the original furniture.

By means of the original ancient stair we enter the atrium of the house, a small quadrangular court, originally decorated perhaps with two statues whose bases can still be seen. On the wall opposite the entrance open the three rooms of the **tablinum** or principal reception room, while on the left there is the *triclinium*, the dining room. The central hall of the tablinum is the one decorated with the greatest care and also the one best preserved. The style of the paintings corresponds to what in Pompeii is called the second style, the style of realistic architecture, since the architecture drawn on the walls could be perfectly well executed in reality, and the perspective is absolutely accurate.

Fig. 27. – Painted interior wall of the so-called House of Livia.

The right wall, the only one whose decoration has been preserved intact is divided by means of columns, cornices and entablatures into several sections (fig. 27). In the central one that is supposed to give the idea of an open window, we see the story of Io, the young priestess of Hera, beloved by Zeus, whom Hera therefore changed into a heifer. A later edition of the myth however relates that the girl was taken to Argos and imprisoned there in the sanctuary of Hera, with Argus Panoptes as jailer, a man of great strength who had a hundred eyes scattered all over his body. However Zeus sent Hermes who was able to slay Argus and free the girl, who, after long wanderings, became a Goddess. Hera placed the eyes of Argus on the tail of her sacred bird, the peacock.

The young beautiful priestess sits at the foot of a column bearing the idol of the jealous Goddess. On the right stands Argus, watching her intently, holding his sword in his hand and with a lance resting on his shoulder. From the left the invisible Hermes approaches swiftly, and looks upward into the heavens in order to receive from Zeus the inspiration and strength necessary to slay Argus.

In the division on the left there is painted a street scene with some tenement houses as a background. A woman knocks at one of the doors, while others come out on the balconies to meet her. The subject is probably simply decorative in object, but is interesting as it shows us the probable appearance of a street in Rome, at that time. The subjects that fill the square high up between the smaller intercolumniations on this wall, and also in the side division of the end wall, are drawn from some unknown mysteries.

The central picture on the end wall has now almost entirely disappeared, but was in a better condition when discovered. It represents the Cyclops Polyphemus following the nymph Galatea into the sea. The nymph is borne on a hippocampus while the giant is playing on the pipes. The floor is still covered with a considerable portion of the original black and white mosaic, the design of which seems to imitate that of a carpet.

The left wing or *ala* of the tablinum is decorated merely with ornamental subjects, placed over an imitation porphyry facing on the walls. The right room however is far more richly decorated and still preserves to a large extent the original freshness of the colours. The wall here is also divided into three sections by means of a feigned portico of Corinthian columns. Between the latter hang magnificent festoons, covered with leaves, fruit and flowers, and embellished with multicoloured ribbons some of which support agricultural implements. The wall behind this portico is divided into white spaces, while above them runs a yellowish frieze. On it is painted in monochrome an " Egyptian landscape " peopled by numerous figures of men and animals (the representation of the camel should be noticed) in the midst of a fertile and varied country.

The paintings in the dining room, the **triclinium,**
continue the motif of the open windows, which was much
liked by the Romans, especially when they did not happen
to possess gardens near their houses. To the right appears a semicircular portico, with statues on the attic;
in front rises a trophy with the spoils of the chase;
while the background is decorated with large branches
that are supposed to be placed not far from the window.
Above the door some fruit is shown in a transparent
glass vase.

The other rooms belonging to the House of Augustus
are undecorated and lie to the southeast of the tablinum.
They are on a higher level and are reached by means of a
stair. They consist of twelve rooms of various size placed
around a kind of central courtyard, rebuilt and restored at
different epochs.

The buildings we have just described formed only
one part of the entire house, to which also belongs a vast
square courtyard to the south. It is very badly preserved
and only appears to have been added by Augustus at a
later date, since it rests on some buildings of late Republican date. There are four tufa pilasters at the corners
and between them bases for columns. This peristyle is
probably that lofty spot where Augustus went when he
wished to deal with secret affairs or to rest undisturbed.
Svetonius (*Aug.* 72) mentions that it was called *Syra-
cusae* and *Techniphyon*, perhaps from its lofty and sunny
position. The road which now divides this portico from

the rest of the house is modern and a poor attempt at a restoration on the part of Rosa.

Having proved that the house we have described is that of Augustus, it is easy to show that the Temple that stands to the south and is usually called the Temple of Jupiter Victor, is really the famous **Temple of Apollo** (12). It was the second building Augustus raised on the Palatine, having been vowed in 36 B. C. and dedicated eight years later. In consequence of the victory of Actium the Temple was often called that of *Apollo Actius* or of *Phoebus Navalis*. It should be mentioned, however, that it is not yet possible to interpret the passages of Ovid or Festus in a manner satisfactory to this attribution. The earlier attribution of *Aedes Jovis Victoris* or *Propugnatoris* (due to the fact that we know that a Temple to this divinity was built on the Palatine by the Consul Q. Fabius Rullianus in 295 B. C. after his victory at Sentinum over the Samnites), is now untenable since the ruins rest on foundations of a house of the last century of the Republic. Moreover the considerable size of the building, (44 metres long and 25 wide) raised on a lofty podium with a majestic approach, as well as the fine *opus quadratum* of marble used to line the concrete core, are strong indications that it is the famous Temple dedicated to the Sun-God, who was also the patron of Poetry and Beauty. His image, which stood in the centre of the sanctuary, between those of his mother Latona and his sister Diana (fig. 28), was an original by Scopas, one of the most celebrated Greek sculptors of the 4ᵗʰ cent. B. C.

Fig. 28. – Diana, Apollo, Latona.
Detail of a monumental base at Sorrento.

To get an idea of the original splendour of the Temple we must turn from the scanty ruins to read the description of Propertius (II, 31). " You ask why I come so late? Great Caesar has opened the golden portico of Phoebus:

wonderful in appearance, spaced with columns of Numidian marble (*giallo antico*), between which sit the innumerable daughters of old Danaus. Here is the marble image of the God, more beautiful indeed than the Sun himself, pouring forth his songs on a silent lyre; and round the altar stands the herd of Myro, four oxen so skilfully fashioned as to seem alive. Then in the center rises the Temple of white marble, dearer to Phoebus than his native Ortygia. Above the pediment of the Temple is the chariot of the Sun, while the doors are a magnificent work of ivory; one represents the Gauls hurled down from the summits of Parnassus, while the other depicts the slaughter of the Niobids. At last, between his mother and sister, comes the God himself, the Pythian master of song, in his long robe ".

The great portico of *giallo antico* was called the **Portico of the Danaids** (14) from the statues of the fifty daughters of Danaus that stood in the intercolumniations, and some of the bases may perhaps be preserved under the Flavian Palace. Behind the Portico stood the two **Libraries,** one for Greek and the other for Latin books, which were famous in antiquity for their order and for the richness of their decoration. A numerous staff took care of the precious volumes.

We must imagine that the Portico of the Danaids and the Libraries were destroyed in the fire of 64 A. D. under Nero, which swept over the whole Palatine, and only spared the western corner. The Libraries were however rebuilt on the same spot by Domitian. We will describe them later (22).

Before leaving the Temple of Apollo we must mention a round marble altar that stands on one of the landings of the great staircase, but that really comes from the other side of the hill where it was discovered in 1868. The inscription mentions a victory of Domitius Calvinus, one of Caesar's generals and consul for the second time in 53 B. C. It says further that with the spoils of this victory (de manubiis) he built or rebuilt the otherwise unknown building to which the altar belonged.

All the Augustan buildings, and especially the Temple of Apollo, were greatly damaged during the fire on the Palatine in 363 A. D., and it seems probable that on this occasion the Temple was entirely destroyed.

4. – THE PALACES OF TIBERIUS AND CALIGULA.

We thus cross the beautiful **Farnese Garden,** laid out by Cardinal Farnese during the middle of 16th century with the help of Antonio da Sangallo, Michelangelo, Vignola, the Zuccari, and the artists of the school of Giulio Romano. The buildings belonging to the Gardens that are still preserved, are the *casino* or aviary, and *the palace*, built on the southern wing of the Flavian Palace, with a loggia decorated by the Zuccari.

The Farnese Gardens may really be considered as hanging gardens supported by the **House of Tiberius** (15),

150 metres long and 120 wide, which is preserved at a height of about 20 metres. Owing to the presence of the gardens it has only been possible to excavate a very small portion of it. On the basis of descriptions of earlier excavations we can perhaps recognize a kind of pillared atrium (A) that stood in the centre of the house and is now covered over. It communicated by means of two stairs (B and C) with the front towards the southeast; the south-western front was formed by the row of rooms (E), built by the Antonines as a guard room for the Praetorians, which we have already described. In the corner (D) there is a fish-pond with stepped sides, where fish for the Imperial table may perhaps have been kept; at the northern corner there is a group of rooms, afterwards hidden in the reconstruction by Domitian after the fire in 80 A. D.

The position of Tiberius' Palace, which rose perhaps on the site of the house where he was born (Svet., *Tib.* 5), is fixed by two passages in Svetonius. In one (*Vitell.*, 15) he mentions that Vitellius, while at dinner was able to see through the windows of the dining room the conflagration of the Temple of Jupiter Capitolinus; in the other (*Otho*, 6) that Otho, in order to get to the conspirators who had gathered in the Forum, crossed the *Domus Tiberiana*, and passed down through the Velabrum. The Palace therefore must have occupied all that side of the Palatine that faces the Capitol and lies between the Velabrum and the Forum, that is to say the side that faces the modern *Via di S. Teodoro*. The library, the *Biblioteca Tiberiana*, connected with the Palace, was very famous. In it were kept the Imperial archives that were burned under Commodus.

All the side of the Palatine that looks over the Roman Forum (16), requires very careful study, since it is very complicated and even now not entirely comprehensible. All this portion was greatly damaged in the two great fires of the first century A. D., that of 64 under Nero and that of 80 under Titus. The latter started on the Capitol, spread to the Forum and gutted all the nothern corner of the Palatine as well, causing special damage to the Palaces of Tiberius and Caligula. On this occasion the House of Tiberius lost its facade on the *Clivus Victoriae* (fig. 29).

Domitian rebuilt the new facade by building a two storied loggia, supported by travertine corbels; there are some remains of the decoration in frescoes and stucco relief. Domitian's successors Trajan, and especially Hadrian, felt the need of increasing the upper surface of the Palace. Thus the former built some great rooms in front of the northern side of the Palace, and the latter built the great arches over the *Clivus Victoriae*, by means of which the front of what had been Tiberius' Palace was brought right up to the Via Nova overlooking the Forum.

Before Nero's fire the *Clivus Victoriae* divided the house of Tiberius from the **Palace of Caligola,** of which we have already spoken in dealing with the so-called Temple of Augustus and the *Atrium Gaii*, its vestibule on the Roman Forum. The classical authors mention with

Fig. 29. – Arcades supporting the Domus Tiberiana
on the Clivus Victoriae

great interest Caligula's works, which extended the Imperial property right up to the Forum. The Temple of Castor and the Temenos of Vesta were incorporated in it and formed a kind of monumental entrance. It is said that the mad Emperor used to stand between the statues of the Dioscuri and receive the adoration of the populace.

The Palace of Caligula is famous as the scene of the murder of that Emperor, in consequence of a conspiracy of some members of his household, headed by the tribunes Cornelius Sabinus and Cassius Chaeraea. On the 24th of January, 41 A. D., Caligula assisted at the preparations or a new performance in a theater nea the *Porta Mugonia*, and afterwards started to return to his House by means of an underground corridor (*crypta*) which was the usual entrance from that side. On the way he stopped to talk with some noble youths who had come from Asia, and who had been placed there expressly with the object of delaying him. As he was talking to the boys, Sabinus, Chaeraea and the other conspirators rushed upon him, and thrust their daggers through him thirty times, all crying out: "Strike again!"

The buildings on the right of the *Clivus Victoriae* up to the summit of the Velia, are very strangely arranged and appear to have been built in two different epochs. The first construction, from the stair *F* to the Farnese aviary, is merely a facade to cover the cutting of the hill where the Palace of Tiberius rose (fig. 30). The rooms are handsome but of uncertain use. The next portion (17)

Fig. 30. — Facade of the Domus Tiberiana on the Clivus Victoriae.

is, on the other hand, a real palace, of which, unfortunately, only the lower floor is preserved. It has a very curious plan.

Before leaving this part of the hill, let us glance at the fountain of the Farnese Gardens, also called the *stanza della pioggia*, which stands at the top of the *Clivus Victoriae*, under the terrace that offers a wonderful view over the Forum. We now enter the underground vaults of the Palace itself, under the Director's house, and reach the **Cryptoporticus of Nero** (19). This wonderful semi-subterranean corridor was intended to connect the Golden House with the Houses of Augustus, Caligula and Tiberius, and it runs all along one side of the latter. An arm was opened later (19, *b*), to put it in communication with the **Palace of the Flavii,** really the work of Domitian alone, who had it built after the plans of his great architect Rabirius. In the section of the cryptoporticus that leads to the House of Augustus may be seen some good stuccos (fig. 31). The vault had been damaged in antiquity and was strengthened by means of pilasters.

5. – The Flavian Palace.

As we mentioned in the introduction to this chapter, this Palace fills the hollow between the *Palatium* and the *Germalus*, and covers the buildings which stood there before. Originally it was all surrounded by porticos, and

Fig. 31. – Stucco decorations of the Cryptoporticus of Nero.

was approached from the side facing the Arch of Titus
by means of a monumental stair, divided into three wide
flights. Classic authors praise, although with nauseous
flattery, the splendor of the Palace. " Nothing so grand
the eye of day sees in all the world! You would believe
the seven hills uprose all together . . . And yet, Augustus,
this Palace that with its pinnacles touches the stars.
though level with Heaven, is less than its Lord ". (Martial, VIII, 36).

The palace of Domitian was despoiled of its marbles
and decorations during the excavations conducted by

8

Bianchini on behalf of Francis I, Duke of Parma, between
the years 1720 and 1722. At that time were discovered
the earlier buildings on which the Palace was built and,
among these, an interesting house of the Republican era
called, with a modern name, *Casa dei Grifi* (about one century B. C.), with paintings of an architectural style (second
Pompeian style) in its earliest period (fig. 32), and a wide
hall which, under the Emperor Caligula, was consecrated
to the worship of Isis (*Aula Isiaca*) as is proved by
the fine frescoes still ornamenting the walls (fig. 33).
Their paintings were copied by Gaetano Piccini, whose
drawings are now in Vienna, and by Francesco Bartoli,
who left 58 large water colours now in the Topham collec-
tion at Eton. In order to give an idea of the splendour of
the Palace it will be sufficient to state that the threshold was formed of one solid block of Greek marble, which
sawn in two, at present forms the high altar in the Pantheon. In front of the door there were two columns of
giallo antico, that have unfortunately disappeared. The
building is divided into three principal parts: the great
reception rooms for solemn functions of State, the peristyle with the bathrooms, and the triclinium with the
fountains (fig. 34).

The reception rooms are three, placed one beside
the other. To the north is the *Basilica* (*A*), also called
the *Basilica Jovis*, which is divided into three naves by
means of Corinthian columns of *giallo antico*, and has
an apse at the end, closed off by a marble screen. It was

Fig. 32. – The large room of the so-called House of the Gryphons.

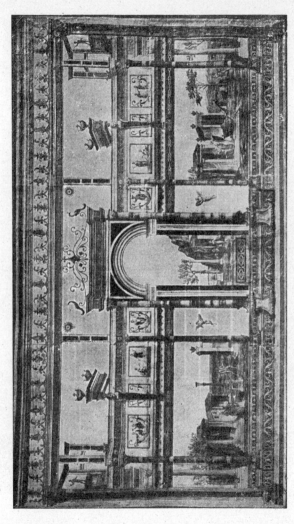

Fig. 33. – Painted interior wall of the Aula Isiaca.

Fig. 34. – Reconstruction of the Palace of the Flavii.

probably used for pleadings before the Emperor himself.
Next comes the *Aula Regia* (*B*), the throne room, a wonderful hall originally decorated with 16 columns of *pavo-
nazzetto* and with 12 black basalt statues in the niches.
Two of these statues were discovered during Bianchini's
excavation in 1724, and were given to the Duke of Parma
and may still be seen in that city. This hall too has an
apse where stood the Imperial throne (*Augustale Solium*)
where the emperor sat to receive foreign ambassadors
and to preside over the meetings of his council. Last is the
Lararium (*C*), the private chapel, in which were kept, above
a small altar, the images of the Penates (the protectors of the
Imperial household), together with those of the Divinities
specially venerated by Domitian, notably Minerva.

From these rooms we pass to the spacious peristyle (*D*),
surrounded by columns of *portasanta* and with a curious
impluvium in the centre, made like an octagonal fountain
with a labyrinth and *jeux d'eau*. Domitian used to like
to walk up and down here, in the shade of the warm
porticos that gave it the name of *Sicilia*. In his dread
of assassination, he had the walls covered with slabs
of *phengites* or marble of Cappadocia, that reflected
like a polished mirror. Thus he was able to see who
approached from behind. To the right of the peristyle
there are some small rooms of curious and elegant
shape (*E*), that have niches and apses for statues and
baths. On the opposite side there are traces of three large
rooms (*F*), perhaps the tablinum with its two wings.

Crossing the peristyle we reach the triclinium or banqueting hall (*H*), the famous *Coenatio Iovis* of the Palatine Palace. It was paved with colored marbles, most of which have disappeared in the hall itself, but are well preserved in the apse, which is raised on a lofty step in order that the sacred person of the Emperor should be removed from contact with the crowd of guests. In the side walls large windows allowed the view of two pretty oval fountains (*G* and *I*) and were later closed. Under and beside the western fountain there has recently been discovered a magnificent pavement in *opus sectile*, belonging to the House of Nero.

Other great colonnades (*L* and *M*) finished the building to the south and west, completing an edifice that led people to say of Domitian that " it is neither piety, nor magnificence, but, indeed, a mere disease of building, and a desire, like Midas, to convert everything into gold or stone " (Plut., *Poplic.*, XV, 7).

Behind the back portico of the Palace (fig. 35) there are some rooms (22) with apses, large rectangular niches in the walls and some steps at the foot of the walls, which prove that they were used as *Libraries*. Since they too were built by Domitian, we must suppose that they took the place of the earlier ones built by Augustus for the Temple of Apollo. Indeed, these rooms seem to fit in better with the orientation of the Temple than with that of the palace.

The excavations executed under the pavement of the *Grand Triclinium* led to the discovery of two groups of

Fig. 35. – Facade of the Palace of the Flavii
facing the Circus Maximus.

monuments of a pre-Domitianic epoch which stood on
the valley lying between the Palatine and the *Cermalus*.
We reach the lowest by means of a stair, lined with marble, beginning on the side of the peristyle next to the
triclinium. At the bottom, built against the front of the
Cermalus, we find a magnificent *Nymphaeum* or ornamental
fountain, partly restored according to the drawings of

1738. The style of the decoration would perfectly agree
with its attribution to the *Domus Transitoria* of Nero,
Behind the nymphaeum there is a network of rooms run-
ning right under the side of the Palace, but their purpose
is uncertain.

The fountain occupies all one side of an open court,
in the centre of which, opposite the fountain, stood a
kind of pavilion, ornamented with columns. The ground
about it was laid our in flowerbeds and fountains, while
a niche in the brick wall was probably for a statue.

All this portion of the *Domus Transitoria*, seriously
damaged by the fire of 64 A. D., was filled in by Nero,
who built the enormous concrete walls to support his
Golden House. These walls were left by Domitian to
strengthen the platform above the hollow between the
two hills.

The pavement of the upper story may be clearly
seen all under Dominitian's triclinium, whose floor,
supported by a number of brick pillars, rests on its bed.
Some traces of the marble pavement are visible behind
the triclinium, under the colonnade. The finest of all
is the superb pavement in *opus sectile of* a porticus, over
which Domitian built one of his oval fountains. The
design is picked out in red and green porphyry and precious marbles on a background of *giallo antico*. A plain-
er frieze ends the design. On either side of the room
stood great columns, the foundations for which are still
visible.

9

6. – The Domus Augustana and the Stadium.

We are in the habit of calling *Domus Augustana* the building standing to SE of the Flavians' Palace, between this and the *Stadium*, which was designed for a private residence of the Imperial family. The palace consists of two different storeys with a relief of 11 metres. The upper storey is formed by two great peristyles of the same axis, of which are visible only the bases of the columns and some traces of the walls belonging to the adjacent rooms. In the middle of the second peristyle there is a large basin in the centre of which we can see the podium of a small, rectangular shrine connected with one side of the portico by means of a bridge with seven arches. The shrine, probably, was consecrated to the protectress deity of the Imperial family. To the south of this peristyle some rooms rise whose extant walls reach up to the second floor. On its side there is the modern building of the *Museo del Palatino* (now closed).

Two grand staircases lead to the lower squared yard (in the center of which a great fountain is visible) furnished with baths, niches and pedestals for statues (fig. 36). A door in the bottom wall gives access to the exedra that formed the front-view of the whole building towards the *Circus Maximus*, originally ornamented with a rich marble colonnade.

The big building, completely coated with precious marbles and statues (mostly the production of the best

Fig. 36. – The lower peristyle of the Domus Augustana.

Greek artists), with golden ornaments, paintings mosaics
and carpetings, must have really become the seat of the
God on the earth, the dwelling of the world-Lord, to
whose worship ambassadors came to Rome from all parts
of the vast Empire.

The STADIUM, or Hippodrome (24), was one of the
most beautifully situated of the monuments on the hill.
It was built, as we have already mentioned, by Domitian
and was surrounded by a portico (fig. 37) with two stories,
which had wide ambulatories inside, and engaged columns
covered with marble on the side towards the arena. At
either end of the arena may be seen the two semicircular
metae, as in a circus, but here they are probably fountains,
since the building must be considered a great garden
and a place where the Imperial family could take exercise,
rather than a ground for actual athletic contests. At the
back of the portico on the left there is a pretty statue of a
Muse, found during the excavations in 1893. Septimius
Severus restored the building, adding the pilasters on the
outside wall and rings to strengthen the vaults.

At the beginning of the Middle Ages, perhaps under
the domination of Theodoric, who dwelt in the Palace of
the Caesars, there was built in the middle of the arena an
oval enclosure, perhaps for games or gardening. It
blocked the curved side of the building and thus altered its original character. In the middle of the stadium there are also the remains of a portico of the late
Empire (C), forming an entrance to an atrium decorated

Fig. 37. — View of the Stadium of Domitian.

with statue bases. In the arena there are many columns of granite and *cipollino* with fine Tuscan capitals, as well as Corinthian and Composite, that probably decorated the various stories of the stadium. There is also a fine square altar on which were originally represented the twelve Olympian divinities. At present there are only Minerva, Juno (?), Demeter, Mars and an arm of Venus.

The **Imperial Box** (25) is of great importance. It is shaped like a great apse, divided into two stories. The lower one has three rooms with very faded paintings. Above was the space where the Emperor could sit and enjoy the view; while behind runs a great corridor with a coffered vault. Below there is another corridor, now dark and full of earth. The back of the exedra is connected with the Baths built by Severus.

One reaches the second story of the Imperial Box by a stair at the southern end of the stadium (*D*), and so we reach the eastern slopes of the Palatine looking towards the valley of the Colosseum and the first spurs of the Caelian. The **Aqueduct** (31) built by Domitian for his Palace and restored by Septimius Severus for his Baths, and of which there are still some arches standing, came up to the Palatine from this side.

The **Baths of Septimius Severus** (26) stand just behind the apse of the stadium, and, for the most part, rest on an artificial plateau, which had been already prepared by Domitian, and was formed by increasing all the southern corner of the hill with enormous substructures (28-29) several stories high. These extended as far as the seats of the Circus Maximus and almost merged into them (fig. 38).

Domitian indeed appears to have had an idea of building some Baths in this spot, as evidenced by the foundations of the buildings itself and from the fact that the aqueduct we have mentioned above (31) is directed here. We do not, however, know why the upper portions only were built, or finished, under Septimius Severus.

7. — THE SLOPES TOWARDS THE CIRCUS MAXIMUS.

Let us now leave the Baths of Severus and the buildings on the summit of the hill, and descend by the way that skirts the Baths on the side of S. Gregorio, and passes under the great arcades. On this part of the hill we must mention a monument that, before it was destroyed in 1589 by Domenico Fontana by order of Sixtus V, stood at the extreme south corner of the Palatine and was famous throughout antiquity and the Middle Ages. According to Spartianus, the **Septizonium** was built by Severus at the furthest end of the Palatine, opposite the Via Appia, in order that the travellers who approached Rome from that side, and especially those coming from Africa, his own birthplace, should at once be struck by the magnificence of the *Urbs Roma* and of its Emperor. It was therefore constructed with special grandeur, and had columns of *antico*, African marble and granite on every

Fig. 38. — Arcades supporting the Palace of Septimius Severus.

floor, and between the columns, apses with fountains and statues. Some drawings of the Renaissance show it in the state it was in before being destroyed, with three floors decorated with columns (fig. 39). Originally it appears to have been seven stories high (*Septem Zonae*) and reached right up to the buildings on the Palatine. Some Medieval documents call it also *Septifolium* or *Sedem Solis* or *Septemsoliis*.

In the archives of the Vatican there are the bills which specify that the destruction of the monument cost 905 *scudi*, but the value of the building material thus obtained was greatly superior and was employed in many of the works of that time. Thirty-three enormous blocks of travertine were used for the foundations of the Vatican obelisk; 104 blocks of marble were employed in restoring the Antonine column and in making the base of the statue of St. Paul; 15 went into the tomb of Sixtus V in St. Mary Major and an equal number into that of Pius V; the columns were dispersed and reworked for numerous churches and chapels.

In the southern corner of the Palatine there are also some traces of buildings (30) of the 2nd or 3rd cent. A. D. but we cannot say whether they belonged to the Imperial buildings. At the foot of the Baths of Severus there is a construction three stories high with windows on the outside, but which is at present much ruined and buried. Under the garden of the Convent of St. Bonaventura (32) there is a neat facade of a house, with brick arches and

Fig. 39. – The Septizonium of Septimius Severus. (Du Perac-Sadeler. 16th century).

pilasters, and with rooms inside, supporting a terrace for a building above, which has disappeared.

Fig. 40. – The *graffito* of Alexamenos
from the Paedagogium.

There is one more monument on the path that runs along the western side of the Palatine below the *Domus Augustana*, known as the **Paedagogium** (39). It was the school for the pages who afterwards became officials in the Imperial bureaucracy. The building itself is of the age of the Flavians, and its purpose is known to us through the numerous *graffiti* that these boys wrote on its walls, especially when they were about to leave it. The most famous is the one now in the National Museum in the Baths of Diocletian (fig. 40). It represents a caricature of the Crucifixion: a figure with an ass's head hanging on the cross and adored by a youth standing on the left. Underneath is written in Greek: "ΑΛΕΞΑΜΕΝΟϹ ϹΕΒΕΤΕ ΘΕΟΝ" that is to say "Alexamenos worships his God'" It is well known that a belief was prevalent among the heathen that the Christians and the Jews worshipped a deity in the form of an ass. This opinion was fostered by the followers of Marcion, the strongly anti-Semite heresiarch who was opposed to the Old Covenant; and by a passage in one of their books, in which mention is made of Zacharias being struck dumb through seeing a man in the form of an ass standing in the Holy of Holies, as given by Epiphanius (*Her.*, XXVI, 12).

A small and dark room, to the left of the principal hall, was perhaps the school prison, since it is particularly covered with inscriptions referring to school life.

Let us go back, now, into the Stadium and remount the staircase situated at the bottom end of the right-side of the portico, up to the *Domus Augustana* and from here go down the Clivus Capitolinus, to the Arch of Titus.

In order to complete the visit of the Palatine, as soon as we come out of the enclosure of the excavation, we take the ascent of San Bonaventura which leads up to the Church of the same name passing between two rows of small chapels (*aediculae*) of the Via Crucis. The Church is built on the great watercisterns of the Imperial buildings, no longer visible. Half-way up on the left side, a wooden lattice gate gives access to the former Barberini vineyard where the Church of St. Sebastian arises, ornamented with interesting mediaeval paintings. In the kitchen-garden of the church we can see the remains of the *Aedes Caesarum* or Temple of the deified emperors erected on the spot where the native house of Augustus arose. Heliogabalus enlarged the temple which, afterwards, took his name. As his biographer states, Heliogabalus collected thereinto all the most important sacred objects of Rome, such as: the *Palladium*, the shields of Mars, and the *lapis niger* (black-stone) of the *Magna Mater*, thus creating something similar to a little Pantheon. All through the Middle-Ages this portion of the Palatine Hill was called " *in Pallara* " (from " *Palladium* ") a name particularly attributed to the little church of *Santa Maria in Pallara* erected among the ruins of the *Templum Caesarum* (Temple of the Caesars).

INDEX

THE ROMAN FORUM

THE PALATINE